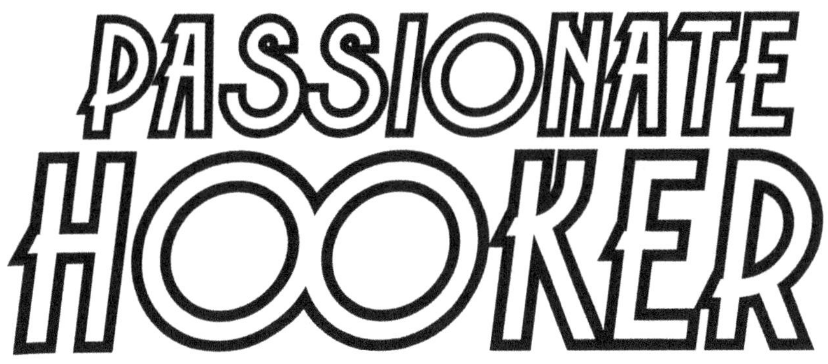
PASSIONATE
HOOKER
(NOT THAT KIND OF HOOKER)

Passionate Hooker

Standing on the Corner of Leadership and Life

Sean Conley

Published by Game Changer Publishing

Paperback ISBN: 978-1-969372-67-4

Hardcover ISBN: 978-1-969372-68-1

Digital ISBN: 978-1-969372-69-8

www.GameChangerPublishing.com

*To Ken, my partner in all things, and to Louis and Winston,
who remind me daily that passion shows up in loyalty,
laughter, and the occasional muddy paw print.*

*To my mentors, coaches, friends, family, work colleagues, and the
thousands who have joined me in workshops over the past forty years—
thank you for shaping this journey with me.*

*And to all the Passionate Hookers out there who dare to lead
with heart and authenticity—this book is yours.*

READ THIS FIRST

Just to say thanks for buying and reading my book,
I would *Love* to connect with you!

Scan the QR Code Here:

SEAN CONLEY

CONTENTS

In the Beginning...   1

1. The Art of Classic Presenting   9

2. Have Heart   23

3. Own Your Brand   33

4. Offer Value   45

5. Keep It Engaging   55

6. Engaging Authentically   67

7. The Three R's   83

8. From Hooker to Hookers   103

9. My Favorite Analogy and Setting Your Intentions   107

Final Thoughts...   123

Sources   129

IN THE BEGINNING...

In all seriousness, this isn't a typical introduction that you can skip. Your "Passionate Hooker" journey starts here, so keep on reading.

Welcome to the world of Passionate Hookers. I'm not talking about the typical kind of "hooker," but rather those who know how to forge genuine relationships and embrace the art of living with passion. Becoming a Passionate Hooker has been a forty-year journey for me, shaped by my experiences and insights, and it has inspired me to write this book.

WHO AM I?

From the very beginning of my career in the hospitality industry, I developed skills that I still rely on today. I started by washing dishes at my parents' restaurant and then branched out to other establishments. I worked multiple jobs to pay rent during my teenage years, all while attending high school and simply trying to survive.

I am grateful for the struggles I've faced, as they have shaped me into the person I am today: hardworking, passionate, and happy with where I am. Working from a young age taught me resilience, the importance of making ends meet, and the survival instinct I carry with me today.

Truthfully, I have never stopped learning and growing, and one of the greatest things I ever learned was that the more I connected with people, the more successful I became.

In my early business years, I discovered my knack for connecting with colleagues, which eventually led me to the world of training and development. This experience is at the heart of what this book is about.

For years, I didn't fully recognize my gift for helping others learn by making concepts relatable and understandable. Many of us go through the day-to-day motions, merely punching in and out without any engagement or passion. With this book, I aim to inspire others who may feel like they've lost their zest for life and work.

As I share my experiences and insights in this book, I promise not to present fancy charts, graphs, or complex statistics. Instead, I'll focus on practical advice drawn from my journey, including classes I have taught for clients, concepts I have learned through numerous train-the-trainer programs, various behavioral assessment certifications I have achieved, books I have read, and podcasts I have listened to. What I will share are simple, actionable steps that can help you show up with more passion.

Throughout your reading journey, I will provide you with various exercises and reflection points. My hope is that you actively engage with this information, as it is designed to support you on your path to becoming a Passionate Hooker.

In my workshops, I have taught these principles and steps to thousands of people around the globe. I often ask, "What is the easiest thing to do with the information I will share with you today?" The answer is... nothing. Doing nothing is super easy and requires zero effort.

So, I pose the same question to all of you: what is the easiest thing to do with the information you read in this book? The answer is simple: nothing. Yep, you can passively read this book, then set it down and do nothing.

Doing nothing requires no effort on your part. Unfortunately, about 99 percent of people who read a book or attend a workshop where they receive valuable information tend to store it in their minds and think, *That was great,* without taking any action. But Passionate Hookers do not settle for that. Passionate Hookers take action.

My encouragement to you is this: as you read through each chapter and encounter a reflection point, pause and reflect on it. When you come across a question, set the book down and take the time to answer it. Allow your thoughts to resonate, and don't hesitate to share your insights with others. By doing so and starting to build new habits, we can truly embody the essence of being Passionate Hookers.

So, buckle up! The insights I share will help you become the passionate connector you're meant to be. I will explain the origin of this concept later in the book, but for now, my goal is for you to engage with others on an ongoing basis and take pride in calling yourself a Passionate Hooker. Together, we can change the way we show up in the world, ultimately transforming the landscape around us.

This journey is much bigger than just me and you. It is about us... our connection with others.

ORIGINS OF A HOOKER

Let's address this right from the start: Yes, I named this book *Passionate Hooker.*

No, it wasn't a typo. When people hear the title for the first time, sometimes they laugh, sometimes they raise their eyebrows (unless they have Botox) at the title, and sometimes they have a blank stare. But you know what? People always react, and I do love getting a reaction.

Many people ask me, "Why this title?" "Why take the risk?" "Why not another title?" or "Why choose a word that makes people feel awkward or surprised?"

Well, my friends, that is precisely the point. In a noisy world, we pay attention to what stands out, what is unexpected, and what has a hook. That's what this book is truly about.

It's about connection, curiosity, and being kind and compassionate toward others. It focuses on how we make other people feel. The title is intentional and playful, with a touch of irony, just like me. But there's more behind the laughter; there's a deeper message.

WHAT'S THE HOOK?

We all strive to make a meaningful impact. We're not just here to talk; we're here to inspire and move others. To truly connect with people, you need to hook them with energy, authenticity, empathy, and a good story.

Truthfully, this book began as a straightforward guide to delivering effective presentations. I initially thought I was writing a manual for those who wanted to gain confidence on the corporate stage, but something bigger kept emerging. I realized this was less about presentation skills and more about life skills. By the way, when I run presentation skills workshops, I refer to people as "hookers," all said with a grin, of course. (More to come on this later, but I wanted you to get a feeling for where this is all going.)

This book is about how we lead, communicate, and create moments that truly matter, whether we're in front of a crowd, working with a team, or spending time with friends and loved ones.

It's about being the kind of person who lights up a room, not by performing but by being genuine. It's about showing up with purpose, not perfection.

It's about choosing passion over polish, connection over control, and heart over hype. The name "Passionate Hooker" stuck because, when you lead with your spark and your heart, you're actually drawing people in with who you are.

You captivate them with your story. You make them want to stay. In a world full of distractions, disconnection, and half-hearted engagement, it's all too easy to just go through the motions without truly engaging. This book is a rebellion against that mindset, a hope for a hooker uprising.

That's right! Let's ignite a hooker uprising with a community of Passionate Hookers. It's a call to be more visible, intentional, and alive.

I hope that this book will be more than just an enjoyable read, that it will become a transformative experience that helps you shift your behavior, reignite your passion, and foster deeper connections with those around you. So, go ahead; read it, live it, and be a proud Passionate Hooker. Take what resonates, make it your own, and disregard the rest.

As you read this book, you will find many questions to answer, a few assignments to do, and things to think about. I call this Hooker Homework or Hooker Habits. So be a good Hooker and do your homework. Yes, it is work, and if you try to implement everything in this book, you will probably feel overwhelmed. Instead, let the ideas marinate a bit. Above all, let's work on how you show up. When you do show up, do it like a Passionate Hooker.

In its earliest use, the term "hooker" wasn't just a euphemism; it referred to someone who had to survive by reading a room, understanding their audience, adjusting their approach, and making quick connections.

There was power in that: a skill, a performance, and, yes, a hustle. While the context may have changed, the underlying behavioral mechanisms remain relevant. In many ways, those early hookers were experts at reading people, understanding something we often forget in business, leadership, and life: you must connect before you can inspire action.

That's the essence of this book. *Passionate Hooker* serves as a guide for how we show up in the world. We want to stop "phoning it in" and hiding behind scripts and start leading, living, and connecting with more passion.

HOOKERS THROUGH HISTORY

Let me take a moment to explore the historical roots of the term "hooker." I conducted extensive research on its origins because you can't have a title like *Passionate Hooker* without understanding the term's significance.

One of the best-known and most widely debated stories associates the term with General Joseph "Fighting Joe" Hooker, a Union general during the American Civil War. According to legend, the camps of General Hooker's army had a rather relaxed moral code, allowing prostitutes to accompany the troops. These women supposedly became known as "Hooker's girls," which eventually got shortened to just "hookers."

General Hooker certainly embodied some of the qualities that the term came to represent: someone who grabs attention, takes risks, and leaves a lasting impression, whether or not they succeed.

However, I conducted a reality check and found that historians generally disagree with the folklore surrounding the term "hooker." The truth is that this term was already in use before General Hooker rose to prominence, particularly in urban areas such as New York.

References to the word date back to the 1830s, where it was a slang term referring to women who lured men off the streets, essentially "hooking" them in. There is even a mention in a 1835 New York article stating, *"The public morals have been shockingly debased by the nightly exhibitions of the hookers in Broadway."*

In this context, the term comes from the verb "to hook," meaning to snag, attract, or seduce, much like hooking a fish. This usage predates General Hooker's rise to fame by decades, as he wasn't a household name until around 1862.

There is another theory that links the term to a notorious neighborhood in Lower Manhattan known as Colyer's Hook. This area had a reputation for poverty, crime, and street-level prostitution in the early 1800s. The theory suggests that prostitutes working around Colyer's Hook were colloquially referred to as "hookers."

Regardless of the origin, one thing is clear: a hooker knows how to grab attention and make a connection, and that embodies the spirit of this book. This book isn't about scandal; it's about skill, specifically the skill of showing up, standing out, and leaving a lasting impression, all while keeping your clothes on. That is the essence of it.

Now, if you are ever on *Jeopardy* or some other game show and a "hooker" question comes up, you have me to thank.

You're welcome!

ONE
THE ART OF CLASSIC PRESENTING

When I began writing this book, I felt conflicted, because my expertise lies in learning and development. For the past forty years, I have dedicated myself to helping people, primarily in the corporate world, enhance their skills. This journey has also led me to become an executive coach and a mentor to many.

Initially, I intended to write a book focused on classic presentation skills and how to present effectively in front of large audiences. Over the years, I have taught presentation skills to clients worldwide, employing a classic five-step approach. These five steps are essential for delivering an impactful presentation, and I did not invent them (they have been around in many cool companies and books for years). In fact, I was taught a variation of them from a company that I worked for.

I also know there are many other models for giving great presentations, but this is the one I use myself and have taught for many years. The point here isn't to debate who has the best model or what makes a great presentation. The point is that this is where I crafted the art of presenting myself.

So, the "classic" presentation skills model would go something like this:

The first step is to **Identify Your Objectives.** This sounds logical, but many people overlook this step. Seriously, to give a great presentation, you must understand what you hope to achieve. I have attended countless presentations where I wondered, *Where is this going, and why am I being talked to about this?* So it's crucial to clearly define your objectives before you begin.

The second step is to **Understand Your Audience.** Once you know your objectives, you must tailor them to your specific audience. People often ask me how I can teach the same material repeatedly. The truth is, I have never taught the same class twice because every audience is unique. You must ensure that your objectives align with those of the audience in front of you today.

With your objectives and audience in mind, the third step is to **Craft Your Message.** The funny part is that this is where many people try to start, a big mistake in my opinion. Crafting your message involves designing your slides and preparing your script, with a focus on delivering your key points effectively to achieve your objectives for your audience.

The last two steps are where I developed my skills as a facilitator. While many people can put words on a page, build a pretty slide, and have a general idea of their topic and audience, they often fail to prepare adequately, so **Be Prepared.** Lack of preparation can lead to fumbling or stumbling in front of an audience.

In my experience as a presentation skills coach (I sound so fancy), I emphasize the importance of practice and being prepared for unforeseen circumstances, such as technical issues and your time being cut (or extended). Your preparation is critical to your success in presentations.

The final component often overlooked by many is to **Present with Confidence.** This includes controlling your breathing, managing nerves, and knowing how to regain your composure if things go awry, such as turning red or stumbling over words.

My favorite part of teaching this model over the years was always the recording of the participants.

Side note: I used to carry around a camcorder and a tripod, and I have to tell you: I love technology. Now, it's all done on your phone.

Everyone would present for a few minutes, and then the other participants and I would give feedback based on what we saw and heard. There was magic in doing this. After several recordings, you could always see a difference; it was amazing.

In summary, the **Five Key Skills for Effective Presentations** are:

1. Identify Your Objectives
2. Understand Your Audience
3. Craft Your Message
4. Be Prepared
5. Present with Confidence

These principles guided my work in corporate training and inspired this book, which began as a simple focus on presentation skills but quickly evolved into a deeper exploration of these essential elements.

PRESENTATIONS AND LEADERSHIP CONNECTION

I started to realize that these five presentation skills were much more than that; they were actually leadership skills. By the way, one thing that I believe is that "Leadership" isn't a title; it is a behavior. I talk about this often in workshops. You can have a fancy title, etc., but leadership is really about how you behave and how you treat others. It is part of the philosophy that drives this book.

Suddenly, I was no longer writing a book on presentation skills. I was writing a book on leadership skills (insert mind-explosion emoji here).

I changed my whole concept, saying, "Okay, let's not write a book on presentation skills. Let's write a book on leadership," because, as a leader, what are your objectives in conversations with your team, supervisor, and clients?

As a leader, who are you speaking to? Are you talking to your direct reports? Are you talking to your peers? Are you talking to investors? Knowing your audience is also really important as a leader.

Well, that leads to the next skill, which is, when you deliver as a leader, what's the message? What are you trying to convey?

And leadership comes in many different forms, right? Sometimes, that message is intended to correct a behavior among team members. Sometimes, it's coaching for performance improvement. Sometimes, that message is connecting with your customers, so they buy more products from you. Therefore, the message is really important.

Then, sure enough, are you prepared to have those conversations? And have you taken some time to actually think about the impact you're making when you talk to people? Preparation is key, just like it is in presentation skills.

The final question is, can you do this with confidence? How do you speak to people with confidence? That doesn't mean with authority, but with care and compassion. And how do you convey a message in a confident way? How do you speak up when things aren't right as a leader?

When I considered all of this, I realized that the art of presentation skills was, in fact, the same as the art of leadership. Then I took it one step further and said to myself, *Well, hold on a second. If presentation skills and how we present information are tied to leadership, then aren't we really talking about life skills?* (Insert another mind-explosion emoji here.)

The answer is a great big YES! Life skills involve considering how you present yourself every day. What are your objectives for today? How do you want to show up? Who are you talking to and showing up for? It might be friends, family members, religious leaders, colleagues, or anyone else. You connect with people all the time. That's your audience.

Then, what's your message? How do you want to deliver things? What are you trying to say to people? Are you prepared to have those conversations and to connect with people? Do you know the art of communicating and making an impact when you communicate there? And, just like in leadership and presentation skills, are you confident in the way that you show up?

I'm sharing all of this with you because I originally set out to write a book that teaches presentation skills. Then it dawned on me that these are, in fact, leadership skills. Finally, coming full circle, leaders are people, and people have lives, so now this is a book about life (insert another mind explosion).

So, wherever you're taking this is really up to you. This information fits in many categories, so whatever it is, you will find your (insert your own mind explosion here).

WHY "PASSIONATE HOOKER"?

Now, I've got to let you in on a little secret. I'd like to share with you where the term "Passionate Hooker" really came from. Many years ago, I was asked to teach a classic presentation skills course in Singapore.

I'd been there several times and had some clients over there. While I was in Singapore, I was actually working with a media company (one that I had previously worked for myself). I was helping all the participants with their pitches, which they would present to their clients to sell their products, get them on air, and generate ad revenue.

I was teaching classic presentation skills, right?

What are your objectives? What are you trying to accomplish here? Who are you speaking to? It's the buyer's this time. What's your message? Are you prepared? How do you approach this with confidence?

Of course, this involved recording people and then providing them with feedback.

There was one participant who was struggling particularly hard. They had the right words and knew what they wanted to say, but they weren't prepared and lacked confidence.

As we watched their recording, I paused it and said, "There's really something missing here." I couldn't pinpoint exactly what it was, until I realized that the missing element was their passion. It was as if they were just going through the motions, presenting timidly and without joy or conviction in the message, with no energy behind the words and no life behind the delivery.

I asked them, "What are you passionate about?" They hesitated and admitted that they weren't passionate about the material. I clarified that I wasn't asking about the material but rather about what they were truly passionate about.

As we took a moment to reflect, they eventually expressed the real things they were passionate about, and from that moment on, everything changed. Facial expressions, hand movements, and energy all transformed; they came alive.

"That's the missing piece. When you connect with people, especially in a sales role (in this case), you need to have that passion to hook them in," I told them. Then I jokingly added, "You need to be a 'Passionate Hooker.'" The room burst into laughter, and I thought to myself, *There's something here.*

From that moment in Singapore, where I witnessed someone who had once been lifeless discover their passion, the concept of being a Passionate Hooker emerged. Reflecting on the importance of being truly passionate, I realized that it involves having zest and excitement for life. Each interaction with people can change the dynamic of the relationship when you infuse it with passion, energy, kindness, and excitement.

PASSION IS LIFE

This approach isn't just about presentation or leadership skills; these are essential life skills that are crucial for success. I often ask people, "What are you truly passionate about?" Most need a moment to think. Rarely do they answer with something like, "Working long hours for insufficient pay." Instead, their passions revolve around meaningful aspects of their lives, such as family, friends, and caring for others.

If you dig deep and connect with the things that truly ignite your passion, you can keep that motivation at the forefront of your mind. Remember, everything you do is for that passion. It's this energy that radiates from your actions.

It's important to note that passion doesn't have to be loud and overwhelming. Sometimes, it's quiet, direct, and forceful. Regardless of its intensity, your passion will evoke a range of emotions, transforming how you connect with others. What matters most is that you embrace your passion, however it presents itself.

When you have passion, it changes everything and influences how you show up each day. Take a moment to reflect on how many times you've shown up without passion or just gone through the motions.

I've found myself falling into that trap many times, but I'm putting this book together not only to remind myself but also to share with others that without passion, you have nothing. It's passion that will drive you and lead you further in your career and in life. Our *human* mission is to cultivate that passion within ourselves and share it with others. If we can do that, we will achieve greatness in leadership and how we present ourselves as individuals.

A TRIP DOWN MEMORY LANE

In recent years, we all experienced a collective event: a pandemic. This was one of the first times in modern history that we all faced the same challenge simultaneously. While this book isn't about the pandemic or anyone's beliefs regarding it, it serves to illustrate a point: in those early days, people exhibited more compassion and connection, largely because we were navigating an uncertain time together.

I remember being in lockdown in my apartment in Hollywood, California, banging my pots at 8 p.m. as a thank you to the health-care and first responders. There was a symphony of beautiful banging pots. While the events happening around the world were very scary and uncertain for me, that moment of gratitude filled my heart with hope.

It quickly became apparent that, as time went on, we fell back into old habits and behaviors. The pot banging dwindled off. I often wondered why this was. Why do we go back to old habits so quickly?

However, I believe we can return to that place of compassion, creating environments—whether at work or in life—where people feel more passionate and empathetic towards one another. This shift will change how we show up every day (so, feel free to bang your pots again).

From my humble beginnings as a presentation skills coach, my goal has evolved from helping people give better presentations to applying that same model to life and leadership. This evolution represents something greater than ourselves. The gift we share by showing up with more passion, even in a fun way, can transform everything we do.

BUILDING HOOKER HABITS

Previously, I mentioned that I would give you some simple exercises to do to start building these habits. Well, here we go. It is time to build your Hooker Habits. Yep, that is how we will refer to them moving forward, so when you see "Hooker Habits," that is your clue to do something.

One Hooker Habit I encourage everyone to try is simple: I define passion as a strong emotion or desire for something. Passion can be grand or small, but it's that motivating force that stirs deep feelings when you discuss it.

Close your eyes for a moment and think about the things you feel strongly about or have a strong desire for. Spend about thirty seconds to a minute reflecting on what drives you and evokes emotion. Once you've identified those things, write them down.

Your passions may include family, friends, religion, education, politics, environmental issues, or any other topic that inspires you.

MY PASSIONS:

____

____

____

____

During my workshops, we would do this same exercise. Then I would have people pair up and share their passion with their partner, one person at a time.

For the first round, I might say something like, "On a scale of one to ten, I felt that at about a 6.25," giving an unconventional number. Then I would have the other partner take their turn. I'd tell them to do the same thing, but this time they would need to amplify their passion to a 25 on a scale of 1 to 10 (you get the idea).

As a result, people would start to exhibit a different energy. You'd notice it on their faces, through their hand movements, and in their overall intensity. All I did was coach them to elevate their passion by reminding them, "I can't feel it. Make me feel your passion. You need to hook me with that passion." The second round of the exercise would demonstrate a dramatic difference in their delivery.

What I want to emphasize is that, as a bystander or audience member, I should be able to feel your passion, whether it's big or small, intense or jovial. It should resonate with the audience from their perspective.

You can also do this exercise on your own. Stand in front of a mirror or share your passion with someone else.

Give yourself some grace as you express yourself, and then ask yourself, *Can I take this to another level?*

The factors that elevate passion include how you deliver it. While the words themselves hold value, the delivery matters greatly. We communicate through body language, words, and the tone of our voice.

PASSION IS MORE THAN JUST THE WORDS

Research shows that body language is the most significant vehicle for communication, especially when sharing passion. This includes facial expressions, hand movements, and overall body movement. The next important aspect is the tone of your voice, which encompasses the highs and lows, loudness and softness, as well as speed and slowness. These elements of tone help bring passion to life. Finally, the words we choose also play a role in making an impact.

When body language, tone, and words align, you create the right setting for someone to feel your passion. It's similar to the saying, "It's not what you said; it's how you said it." For instance, someone could say, "I'm sorry," but if they have their arms crossed, are tapping their foot, and have a scowl on their face, the message doesn't come across as sincere. The mismatch between words, body language, and tone leaves the listener feeling unconvinced.

So, we need to unify these elements. By using your body, tone, and words effectively, you can begin to share your passion. This exercise can be done by writing down your passions, reflecting on them, and asking yourself questions like, *What would my body look like? How would my voice sound? How can I choose the right words to convey my message?*

Understanding these elements is the first step toward being more passionate and connecting with others. This is your hook to draw people in. This is how you become someone who genuinely inspires passion: by harmonizing body language, tone, and words with the energy of what you are passionate about.

I can attest from my own experience, having conducted this exercise in Singapore and numerous times with people from diverse cultures around the world, that it is effective across all backgrounds and age groups. Ultimately, we are simply trying to make connections with others.

I firmly believe we truly live in a heartfelt and compassionate world. Yes, there are many people, politics, disagreements, differing views, and unkindness around... but in my heart, I know there is more good than bad. It is just that the bad or negative often gets amplified with anger (just another form of passion).

I also believe that the rise of technology has negatively impacted our communication skills. Many of us have become somewhat lazy and have lost the passion we once brought to our interactions. Think about it; most of us have attended meetings on platforms like Teams, Zoom, or Webex.

During these meetings, it's common for people to leave their cameras off. When your camera is off, we lose the ability to see and feel your body language, which is a crucial part of effective communication.

I've heard every reason for not turning on cameras, but I believe these are just excuses. The truly passionate and committed individuals always turn on their cameras during virtual meetings. This allows them to convey their emotions through facial expressions and tone of voice, enhancing their message's impact.

We have all also seen people sitting together and just texting away, not even speaking to one another, and people walking down the street with their heads buried in their phones. Does anyone stop to enjoy the beauty around us anymore?

HOOKER HABIT

Take a fifty-nine-minute technology break each day during your working hours. Discover what it is like to be technology-free.

Write down your feelings here:

____

____

____

____

How can you incorporate this into your daily life?

____

____

____

____

Passionate Hookers stand out; they take initiative and set examples for others. Whether in person or virtual, these skills are vital in every situation we encounter. Let's not allow the complacency of others to become our excuse.

In the following chapters, we will look at each letter of the HOOKER acronym in a bit more detail:

H   **Have Heart:** Lead and live with passion and purpose, because people are drawn to leaders/people who genuinely care.

O   **Own Your Brand:** Be intentional about how you show up; your reputation is built by every choice you make.

O   **Offer Value:** Focus on giving before getting, creating connections through generosity and substance.

K   **Keep It Engaging:** Bring energy and creativity that invite others to lean in, feel included, and stay involved.

E   **Engage Authentically:** Drop the mask. This authenticity builds trust faster than any polished performance.

R   **Relax, Reflect, Reward:** Sustain your passion by pausing to breathe, reflecting on the journey, and celebrating along the way.

TWO
HAVE HEART

In this chapter, we will explore the meaning of the acronym HOOKER. To kick things off, the "H" represents "Have Heart."

I've spent quite a bit of time reflecting on this concept, and I believe it's only fitting to share a personal story about my cardiologist (no better connection to heart than with a cardiologist) because, without heart, we truly have no hope.

Years ago, a few days into a trip to Kuala Lumpur to teach a class, I began to feel dizzy and lightheaded. Even though I wasn't feeling my best, I pushed through and continued teaching, unaware of how serious my condition was. It wasn't until the final day of class that I truly realized something was off when I felt as though the room was literally turning upside down. I had to pause, take a seat, and fan myself, and in that moment, I understood that something wasn't right.

The next day, I was scheduled for a long flight home, but I thought I was simply dealing with an ear infection. To be safe, I visited a nearby medical center, explained my symptoms to the intake specialist, and anxiously awaited my results. After taking my blood pressure, she handed me a note and said, "You need to get in a cab right now and go to the hospital. Give them this piece of paper."

In that moment, a wave of anxiety washed over me. Everything was happening so swiftly! I hopped into a cab, headed for the hospital, handed over the note, and was ushered into a patient room almost immediately. Suddenly, I found myself connected to medical equipment, and my situation escalated beyond anything I had imagined. I had thought it was just a minor ear issue, and now I was being admitted to a hospital in a foreign country, all alone.

Despite the fear, I was grateful for the support of my colleagues who came to my aid during that difficult time. Eventually, a doctor walked in and introduced himself as a cardiologist. He explained that there was an issue with one of my heart valves and that I would need open-heart surgery. Hearing those words while away from home filled me with panic and a storm of thoughts.

However, he reassured me, saying, "We're going to make sure you're stable enough to fly home. You can have the surgery in your own country; that will make recovery easier." I was still trying to grasp the reality of the situation, absorbing his words with a mix of disbelief and anxiety. They started me on blood pressure medication to prepare for my flight, and I ended up spending two nights in the hospital until they felt I was okay to fly.

The day after landing, I quickly arranged an appointment with a cardiologist whom a family member had previously seen. When I entered his office, the doctor, who appeared relatively young, asked, "What seems to be the problem?" I handed him the paperwork from Kuala Lumpur, and my heart raced as he reviewed the details.

He looked up and calmly stated, "It looks like you need open-heart surgery. It's pretty routine." At a loss for words, I simply nodded as tears began to well up in my eyes. Noticing my reaction, the doctor frankly and unemotionally asked, "Why are you crying? I just told you it's routine."

"It's just a lot to process," I managed to reply.

He said, "You can schedule with the front office, and I will see you once we start treatment," and he left the room. I was treated like a "number," not a person. I left his office feeling overwhelmed and somewhat dazed.

Fortunately, I had discussed my situation with a client who encouraged me to seek a second opinion from a different doctor, let's call him "Dr. S.," who was affiliated with a very famous hospital. Feeling hopeful about this suggestion, I made an appointment with Dr. S. As I walked into his office, a hint of worry still lingered, but I knew I had to keep my heart and mind open to the possibilities ahead.

After I shared my story, Dr. S. gently said to me, "Wow, that must've been really scary." In that moment, I realized what it means to have *heart*. He didn't focus on processes or fear; he connected with the human side of the situation. He genuinely acknowledged my fear, and I affirmed that it was indeed scary.

Then he assured me, "Well, I'm here to help you. I'll take care of this, and we'll figure everything out." I didn't share this story just because it relates to my experience with my heart. I shared it because when I thought about the origins of "having heart," the first person who came to mind was this compassionate cardiologist. Unlike many others in his profession, he took the time to care about the human sitting in front of him.

Whenever I discuss being a passionate leader and emphasize having heart as the first part of this acronym, it reflects the importance of genuinely caring for people. It's about the connections we have. This ties back to the previous chapter about classic presentation skills: do you care about the people you are speaking with, your audience? Do you care about your team, your business, and your clients? In life, do you truly show up with heart and care for others?

To me, this connection is crucial. If you remember nothing else from this book, remember that how you show up and the care you bring to others changes everything. In researching this topic, I posted the following question on LinkedIn: *"What does it mean for a leader to have heart?"* I received numerous responses. Comments included empathy, commitment, trust-building, caring, delivering impactful messages, kindness, and sympathy—you get the idea.

This reminded me that while we may use different terms, having heart ultimately means showing up for the person in front of you and genuinely caring about them. When you can connect with people this way and bring passion into your interactions, you are on your way to becoming an unstoppable leader, friend, family member, or supervisor. Yes, and an unstoppable, Passionate Hooker! We need to bring heart into everything we do.

You can call it what you want; I simply refer to it as care. I am thankful to Dr. S. for the compassion he showed me during that process. By the way, I ultimately didn't need open-heart surgery; we used a different technology that he cared enough to explain. This approach was actually quite fascinating from a scientific and medical perspective. Yes, I do have a fancy new heart valve. However, I would never have learned about it had I gone with the first doctor, who didn't care and lacked heart.

Let me share a couple of examples to illustrate the importance of caring and see if any of these resonate with you. How many times have you been with someone, whether at work or around the dinner table, having a conversation while they are distracted by their phones or other technology? We often pretend to connect while merely sending messages to others, missing the point of genuine interaction. I have been guilty of this as well, and I have to remind myself that this behavior does not reflect true care.

We may have lost the art of genuinely connecting with people. Often, we're simply "human *doings*" rather than "human *beings*." We are busy with our tasks, going through the motions. Having heart means connecting with people, which requires putting down your technology. When participating in a virtual meeting or gathering, engage fully: turn on your camera, maintain eye contact, and have meaningful conversations with others. This shift can change everything. "Having heart" is about being fully present. We must overcome the bad habits we've developed in this regard.

As I reflect on the importance of having heart in how we show up in our interactions, I'm reminded of a book from the 1980s called *Moments of Truth*, by Jan Carlzon, who was involved in the airline industry. The central premise of the book emphasizes that every interaction we have truly matters. Each of these interactions is referred to as a "moment of truth." We have numerous daily interactions, and each one presents an opportunity to connect with others.

Although the book primarily focuses on customer service, I applied its concepts during my early career at a restaurant company, where I served as a trainer. I found myself teaching new food servers how to create their own moments of truth.

In these moments, you face a choice: do you look the other way, or do you help others? It's interesting to me that even after forty years, I am still discussing this topic because it has a significant impact.

Whether you interpret moments of truth through the lens of customer service or personal connections, every interaction is important. For example, I remember my first visit to a cardiologist's office, where I felt like just an insurance number, a mere process to check off. In contrast, there was a moment in Dr. S's office when he acknowledged my feelings by saying, "That must have been scary." This was a moment of truth that created a lasting relationship, whereas the first instance had a negative impact, even resulting in a loss of business.

HOOKER HOMEWORK

What does "having heart" mean to you? For our next exercise, take some time to reflect on what those words evoke. Does it signify care, compassion, trust, or empathy?

____

____

____

____

How can you ensure that in every interaction, every moment of truth, you embody those qualities?

____

____

____

By recognizing that every moment matters, you can shift how you engage with others, whether as a leader, parent, friend, partner, or supervisor.

COMMUNICATION AND IMPACT

To truly have heart, we must let go of habits that have held us back. A key aspect of this is being more present in our interactions. Additionally, it's vital to acknowledge how we communicate with others. Previously, we discussed the impact of communication, which is conveyed through our body language, tone of voice, and the words we use. However, body, tone, and words are the ways in which we make an impact when we communicate.

When we communicate, we are really only doing one of three things: telling, asking, or listening (this comes from the many workshops I have taught).

Often, we engage in communication simply by sharing information with others, opening our mouths and producing sound, words, and sometimes just noise. Whenever you send an email, text, or other message, you are conveying a specific meaning. We are constantly inundated with others telling us what to do. Telling is really at the core of most businesses, by the way. Typically, in business, you are telling someone to do something, such as buy your products or engage with your services. Please don't get me wrong. Telling is a critical part of communication; it's just not the only part.

There are two additional forms of communication: asking and listening. While telling is about pushing out information, a more heartfelt approach involves asking others for their opinions and thoughts. This method brings people into the conversation and creates connection.

Without delving into the details of open-ended and closed-ended questions, the key takeaway is that involving others through inquiry allows you to engage with heart and passion.

However, the true essence of having heart in our interactions lies in mastering the art of listening. It's essential to recognize the difference between genuinely listening and merely waiting for your turn to speak.

SOMETHING TO THINK ABOUT

How many times have you gone through the motions of listening? You might look people in the eyes, nod as they're talking, and perhaps write things down or make noises like "uh-huh," "that's great," or "that's interesting." Meanwhile, in your head, you're doing something else. We call it multitasking in today's world, but you're not really engaged, and you're not truly listening.

Having heart means understanding that telling is about pushing information, while asking is about pulling information. To genuinely develop those heart skills, you need to listen to people. Regarding my cardiologist experience, the first doctor never listened; he simply followed a routine. The second one, Dr. S., actually listened to me and said, "That must have been really scary." That's the difference.

If you have heart and you recognize where your passion originates, you'll understand that every interaction is a moment of truth. Think about your own moments of truth. Don't go through the motions of connecting with people; genuinely engage in conversations because you care about them. Build trust, show empathy, and practice kindness.

The first step on the journey of becoming a Passionate Hooker is to "Have Heart." So, what are some things you can do to demonstrate that you have heart? This applies to showing yourself compassion just as much as it does to showing compassion for others.

HOOKER HOMEWORK

Now that you understand the concept of having heart, here are some actions for you to take.

While the previous exercise is very similar to this one, here's the difference. The previous exercise is a general statement: what comes to mind when you think of the term "Have Heart"? *This* exercise is now specific to *you*.

What does it mean for *you* to "Have Heart"? Write down all the words you associate with having heart.

____

____

____

____

Reflect on improvement. Consider the words you wrote above: what can you do to improve in these areas? For example, if you wrote down "trust" but you're not demonstrating trustworthy behavior, think about how you can change that. Make the connection between your definition and your actions.

____

____

____

____

You know what your definition is. Now your task is to incorporate those principles into your life so you can genuinely show up with heart.

THREE
OWN YOUR BRAND

When I talk about owning your brand, I am reminded of a story. A few years ago, I was traveling, and while at the airport, someone suddenly looked at me and said, "I know you. I recognized you because of your hat. Is your name Sean?" To my surprise, this person told me, "I was one of your students."

My first thought was, *Wow, what are the odds of this happening?* I was in an airport, and someone randomly recognized me. (Fun fact: this is the second time someone recognized me while traveling. My hats really do give me away!)

We had a brief conversation, during which they said, "I learned a lot from your class. I gained insight about communication, but more importantly, I learned a lot about myself." They went on to say that they felt they had become a better coach and people leader and that their team looked up to them now.

As I reflect on the idea of owning your brand, this story resonates with me. Both that person and I navigated what we call personal branding. A **Personal Brand consists of Four Components:**

1. Knowledge and what you do with it. The student I met raised their knowledge through attending my workshop. I, too, was working on my knowledge by conveying information effectively. By reading this book, you are building more knowledge.

Consider whether the information you are reading is new to you or a refresher. If it's new, think about how you will apply it. If it's familiar, ask yourself why you haven't yet acted on it. Always strive to use what you learn. Build your knowledge, and then apply it.

2. How you show up. The student became a better people leader because they learned to present themselves more effectively. Similarly, I aimed to deliver information in an experiential way, which contributed to my image as a facilitator.

How you show up goes beyond physical appearance, though that is important in many corporate and business settings. How you show up encompasses the relationships you build and the connections you establish with others.

It also involves your communication skills, as mentioned in the previous chapter. How do you ask questions? How well do you listen? Are you striking the right balance in your communication? Additionally, your demeanor and poise significantly impact how you present yourself in social and professional situations.

3. What you leave behind. The third component is what people remember about you and what they say regarding your reputation. It's clear that my reputation (what I left behind) was positive since this person approached me to share their experience.

Consider how you say things, when you say them, and what characteristics you bring to the table. Often, our reputation reflects what we do when no one is looking. Be better at asking for feedback, listening to it, and taking action. Your reputation consists of the impressions and thoughts others have when you leave the room.

Just like in my story about passing through an airport, someone reached out to me because of my reputation. They felt compelled to connect with me, hoping I would remember them or that I was the person they were thinking of. My reputation left a mark on this person, as I'd helped them on their journey to becoming a leader. Similarly, your personal reputation is like a company's—you own it.

Think about that. How do you act when no one else is around or when you don't think anyone's watching? That is what your reputation truly represents.

At work, your reputation is closely tied to the quality of your work, not just the quantity. In your personal life, it's not about how many people you know but the quality and depth of the relationships you have with them. We often boast about the number of connections or followers we have on various social media platforms. While the numbers might be significant, the depth of the relationship is missing. Yet people flock to be followers instead of making their own positive mark.

4. Are you being seen? Finally, the last aspect of personal branding is about being seen. I consistently wear hats, which has made me recognizable.

In the crowded airport, one of my distinctive hats helped me stand out, allowing my former student to recognize me. I do like being known as "the guy with the hat" because it means that part of my brand visibility is working; it is a recognizable part of who I am. (Shameless plug here: shout out to Goorin Brothers Hat Makers, whose hats I have been wearing for years.)

Just as companies need visibility to thrive, we, as individuals, also need to be recognized. If we're not seen, others may forget about us. Thus, being visible and actively participating in various settings, such as at work, social events, sports, school, and meetings, is vital. Raising your hand and volunteering can be challenging, but it's a great way to enhance your visibility.

Work on your net*worthing* skills.

Side note: I don't use the word "networking." I use "net*worthing*." Every opportunity you have to engage with others is a chance to enhance your personal brand's worth.

When attending conferences or social gatherings, do you engage with others, or do you stay at the back and wait for them to approach you? To develop your personal brand, you must take the initiative and be visible. Your knowledge, how you present yourself, how people remember you, and whether you are being seen, all contribute to the makeup of your brand.

To own our personal brand, we need to understand and embrace all these elements: our knowledge, how we show up, what we leave behind, and being seen. It's essential to recognize that we are our brand. Just as companies have their brands, every person does, too.

COMPANY BRANDS AND PEOPLE BRANDS

A company's brand represents its identity as presented to the public. Similarly, our personal brand encompasses our unique skills, life experiences, and personality, what makes us who we are and how others perceive us.

Company brands are owned by many people, including shareholders, investors, and employees. In contrast, your personal brand is entirely yours. It encompasses your values, beliefs, and experiences, all of which shape who you are. You are the sole owner of your personal brand.

Companies have brands, and they use various marketing strategies, advertising slogans, and public relations efforts to attract customers and investors. However, your personal brand is about how you present yourself. It's your storytelling and how you demonstrate authenticity in everything you do.

Company brands aim to entice people to shop, spend money, and attract new investors and customers. Personal brands function similarly: your goal is to connect more effectively with your peers, supervisors, partners, parents, and teachers. These interactions help others understand and appreciate your brand.

Like company brands, personal brands require you to take an active role in your own marketing efforts. Both types of brands need constant attention and effort to develop and maintain their value. Your brand is built over time, but it can also be easily damaged. Everything you do contributes to protecting that image.

HOOKER HOMEWORK

Write down the names of company brands that you admire. Consider the companies you respect and enjoy supporting.

____

____

____

____

After listing these companies, reflect on why you admire them. Is it due to their ease of use, the quality of their products, or their contributions to society?

____

____

____

____

Next, let's apply this exercise to your personal brand.

Think about people, living or deceased, fictional or real, whose brands you admire. Write down their names.

Just as you did for the companies, ask yourself why you chose these individuals. Is it their presence, the words they use, or the work they do that inspires respect?

By engaging in this exercise, you can gain valuable insights into both company and personal branding, helping you to understand and enhance your own unique brand.

You've created a list of companies and people you admire, along with the reasons for your admiration. I would like you to review the words you've written and categorize them according to the four key elements I mentioned earlier. Consider whether the qualities you noted are attributable to the knowledge or competence of the individuals or companies.

Did you admire those people or organizations because of their knowledge or skill? Did their image, how they present themselves, or how they connect with you influence your admiration? Were your impressions based on their reputation and the way they have interacted with you? Or did you base your admiration on the visibility and public perception of the company?

As you review your list, you'll likely find that everything falls into one of those four categories. This process helps us work on our personal brand by recognizing what we admire and applying it to ourselves. The first element of our brand is knowledge.

HOOKER HOMEWORK

What are people saying about your personal brand right now? Take some time to jot down your thoughts.

Where do you want your personal brand to be? What might be holding you back?

By identifying what people are saying about you and envisioning your desired brand, you can recognize what may be hindering your progress in developing your personal brand.

As you think about this, I recommend recording yourself. Use your phone to video yourself as you talk about your brand and answer these questions: What is my brand? What do I want my brand to be? What will I work on? After a few weeks, revisit that recording to assess your progress on your journey to improving your personal brand.

Here are a few additional exercises and strategies to help enhance your personal brand:

- Honestly assess your strengths and areas for improvement.
- Seek feedback from others about how you're presenting yourself in both personal and professional environments.
- Consider getting a mentor or coach who will provide you with candidness and guidance.
- In today's digital age, be mindful of your social media presence. Ensure that your online brand accurately reflects the positive image you want to convey. This includes being cautious about what you post, as every tweet, text, or message contributes to your brand.
- Finally, evaluate how you net*worth* and engage with others, not only in formal settings like conferences but also in general life interactions. Are you truly connecting with people?

A FEW PERSONAL REFLECTIONS ON OWNING YOUR BRAND

The first time I recognized I had a personal brand, I didn't really label it that way. After I had finished a presentation for a group of new leaders, one of them approached me and said, "Gosh, I really want to be just like you. You're unmistakable." At that moment, I thought they were just being kind, but that word, "unmistakable," stuck with me.

It wasn't about my clothing (although I do dress cool) or my presentation slides (yes, they were fantastic); it was about how I showed up and delivered my message.

Here's the truth: whether you like it or not, you already have a personal brand. The real question is, are you owning it, or is it owning you?

In every room you enter, every meeting you attend, and every conversation you have, people are picking up on your energy and presence. I refer to that as your brand. They're forming a narrative about who you are, what you stand for, and whether you are someone they want to follow or collaborate with.

Your personal brand is not defined by your job title, your resume, or even the logo on your business card. It's the impression you leave behind when you exit a room. If you don't define your brand, others (your audience, your team, or your peers) will do it for you.

We've all encountered someone whose brand has gone awry, someone who is reactive instead of intentional. They might be competent or even brilliant, but they never take the time to consider, *What do I want to be known for?* As a result, they become generic, forgettable, and just another name in an organization.

A Passionate Hooker approaches this differently. They take ownership; they don't leave their brand to develop by chance. They shape it with purpose. They communicate in a voice that is unmistakably theirs and carry themselves with confidence, clearly knowing who they are.

Owning your brand matters now more than ever in our noisy world. When you take ownership of your brand, you give people something to connect with. You become magnetic. You become unmistakable. You become the person you aspire to be. You don't need to seek attention or validation; people are drawn to you because they understand what you stand for. This fosters trust, builds connections, and creates momentum.

Owning your personal brand isn't about performance or perfection; it's about alignment between who you are, how you act, and what you value. When these elements are in sync, people will notice, listen, and engage.

You are not here to blend in; you are here to show up fully, boldly, and passionately, and it all begins with your brand.

FOUR
OFFER VALUE

We've discussed the importance of having a heart and owning your brand. The connection between your brand and how you present yourself reflects your heart. The second "O" in HOOKER stands for how you "Offer value."

A few years ago, I was on a flight from New York to Los Angeles, which took about five and a half hours. Sometimes, when I board a plane, I'm in the mood for quiet time and love to just look out the window. Other times, I'm curious about the people around me and enjoy engaging in conversation. It really depends on how I'm feeling that day.

On this particular flight, I was hoping for a quiet trip to LA. I had chosen a window seat, and when I arrived, the person next to me was already seated. I approached him and said, "Excuse me. I need to sneak in there; that's my seat." The gentleman stood, and I noticed he was well over six feet tall and had a solid build. He was wearing camouflage fatigues and seemed to have a big presence, but he was also very kind and smiled as he said, "Oh, no problem."

Once I took my seat, the flight attendant came by to offer drinks. I decided on a glass of champagne, and the man next to me ordered a beer. I commented on how refreshing his beer looked, and he returned the compliment by saying my champagne looked good, too, although a little "froufrou" (I swear that is what he said). From that moment on, we talked for the entire five and a half hours.

I share this story because, at first glance, we seemed very different from one another, even from our choice of drinks. As our conversation progressed, I learned about his trip. He was traveling through Los Angeles to head to Australia for a big game hunt. He collected trophies from his hunts, and he displayed the heads of the animals he had hunted back home. He then showed me pictures on his phone.

I then told him I am a vegetarian.

As a vegetarian, I felt sad hearing about his kills and seeing the pictures that he was so proud of. One reason I chose vegetarianism is my love for animals, so it pains me to think about hunting for sport. I expressed my feelings to him, saying, "That makes me really sad." He acknowledged our differences and explained that he always hunts in impoverished areas, like the Australian outback, and donates the carcasses to the local villagers for food.

While I still don't condone big game hunting in any form, I respected his reasoning and his efforts to help others. We also discussed politics and realized that we came from very different sides of the political spectrum.

We couldn't have been more opposite, yet we engaged in open discussions about our views, striving to understand and learn from one another without judgment. We had fun along the way.

During our conversation, he learned that I am gay, while he is straight and has children. He said, "Normally, I wouldn't talk to people like you," but then he added that he was glad we were talking now. I replied that I might not have initiated a conversation with him, either, based on his appearance and the judgments I had made about what he was wearing.

I share this experience because it was real and impactful. Our discussion included topics such as politics, my sexuality, his grandchildren, dietary choices (like being a vegetarian versus a meat-eater), and even hunting. Throughout it all, we maintained respect and kindness. By the end of the flight, I considered him a friend, and I felt we had changed each other's lives for the better by sharing meaningful moments together.

When the plane landed, we were still talking, and a flight attendant remarked, "I didn't think you guys would ever stop talking." We both laughed, realizing we had already arrived. As we exited the plane, we shook hands, not exchanging contact information, but rather, exchanging a friendship. We touched each other's lives in a profoundly magical way.

This experience inspired me to share my story about offering value in relationships. When I speak of value, I don't mean monetary value; instead, I'm referring to the value found in presence, intention, and connection. Offering value means contributing meaningfully to someone else's moment. In this exchange, I wasn't the only one providing value; he offered it to me as well. He listened, was kind, and showed genuine interest, just as I did for him.

In a world where we often discuss networking in transactional terms, it's essential to remember that real value goes beyond mere exchanges. This is why I call it "Net*worthing.*"

Years ago, I worked for a theme park. When I attended traditional networking events, people would approach me and pretend to care about my work, but their primary interest often seemed to be obtaining free tickets, which I found selfish. That's not the kind of value I aim to provide. Situational value, where people use you for their own interests, thereby diminishes your own value, or the value they perceive you to have.

Consider how you show up in conversations. Your value lies in making others feel seen, heard, and supported. That's what happened during my flight. We both felt seen, heard, supported, and valued for who we are, differences and all. The true value you bring to any situation is felt rather than measured. After that experience, I understood how important both he and I were in that moment (our Moment of Truth). It changed me forever, prompting me to reflect on how others feel after our conversations.

To truly offer value to people, begin by being curious. Avoid trying to control the situation; instead, ask better questions that delve deeper than superficial topics.

Sentences like "Help me understand," "Tell me more about that," and "I'm really interested and would love to know more," are fantastic ways to spark conversation and engage with others. It's important to remember, as you listen, that you may not agree with everything you hear. However, you're gaining insight into someone else's experiences and life journey, which ultimately shapes who they are.

When you offer value in a conversation, remember that you are not only sharing your perspective but also receiving valuable insights from others. It's crucial to make your interactions about the other person rather than just yourself. Allow others the chance to shine and be in the spotlight; your turn will come. Be mindful not to always raise your hand and speak first, as this can shut down others' contributions. Instead, invite them to participate.

As a leader, consider the following when trying to add value to your team: be present, connect emotionally, and listen intently. Listening should be genuine, aimed at building trust rather than simply waiting for your turn to speak. Recognize that everyone brings their whole self to work, encompassing struggles and successes. Encourage sharing of both, making room to celebrate personal achievements while also acknowledging challenges. Focus on the person behind the job, not just the job metrics and performance.

Beyond the workplace, strive to offer value without expecting anything in return. Approach connections with openness, kindness, and attention. Enjoy the process; the joy you bring can enhance your relationships. Use humor and light-hearted jokes about yourself to make your interactions more relatable and human.

Listening, often overlooked, is a vital skill in an age when people frequently engage with their devices rather than with each other. We must learn to connect more meaningfully. Remember that everyone wants to feel heard, and you can offer that value by letting others express themselves.

Not every moment of offering value has to be grand. Sometimes, it's as simple as a conversation. I remember reconnecting with a friend I hadn't seen in years. We met over dinner at a beautiful hotel here in Las Vegas—good food, a Cosmo (or two), you know, the kind of setting that invites you to slow down and just be present.

What struck me wasn't the meal (which was awesomely overpriced) or the surroundings (which is why the meal was overpriced)—it was the exchange. We both had so much to share, but neither of us dominated. We listened. We laughed. We touched on the lighthearted moments and the life-changing things we have been facing. And in that back-and-forth, we both felt heard, respected, and engaged.

That dinner reconfirmed to me that value isn't always measured in information, expertise, or big gestures. Sometimes the deepest value we can offer is simply making space for another person's voice, giving them our curiosity, and being fully present.

Is it just me, or do so many conversations often feel imbalanced? One person talks, the other nods, and the "exchange" becomes one-sided or worse yet... no-sided.

But the value multiplies when both people show up intrigued, listening, and contributing. It's not about walking away with answers, but with connection.

Side note: Go to any restaurant and watch people have a meal together. What you typically see is people on their phones and not even being present (yes, I am older and, yes, I know age is a number, but my number is getting higher), but I remember when there was joy and conversation around the table.

That dinner also reminded me of what leaders often miss: the power of being fully present in conversation. Too many one-on-ones become status updates, data dumps, or rushed check-ins between meetings. The task gets covered, but the person doesn't feel seen.

As leaders, one of the greatest values we can offer isn't an answer, a strategy, or a solution—it's presence. It's slowing down long enough to ask, "How are you doing, really?" and then listening with genuine curiosity. It's letting silence stretch a little, so the other person knows their voice matters.

When people feel heard, they feel valued. And when they feel valued, they engage more deeply. The impact isn't just a better meeting; it's stronger trust, greater commitment, and a culture where people bring their best because they know it matters.

Offering value as a leader doesn't always come from the big moves. Sometimes it's found in those small, meaningful exchanges where you put the phone down, close the laptop, and give your full attention. Just like that dinner conversation, the simple act of truly connecting can change the dynamic completely.

HOOKER HOMEWORK

Think back to a recent conversation you had—whether at work or in your personal life. Did you truly slow down and listen, or were you more focused on responding, rushing, or moving to the next task? How might the other person have felt in that moment?

Now imagine a "do-over." If you had that same conversation again, what would you do differently to make the other person feel more heard and valued? What questions could you ask, or what space could you create, to turn it into a richer exchange?

Consider each interaction as an opportunity to make someone's day a little better, especially during challenging times. Reflect on how you can enhance the human experience in these interactions. By doing so, you will stand out and genuinely add value to others. It's essential to think about what you bring to every situation and how you approach connections and relationships. Focus on giving, rather than receiving, the gift of your presence, and foster real, lasting relationships.

Offering value is part of our shared journey in this collective experience.

I once attended a Coldplay concert, despite not considering myself a big fan (at the time, but I am now). This experience reinforced the importance of being open to new connections and moments that can enrich our lives.

Initially, I wasn't familiar with Coldplay's music. It wasn't that I wasn't a fan; I just didn't know much about them. However, I'd seen a few clips of their performances, and everyone said they put on a spectacular show, so I decided to give it a try.

Sometimes the value is in the experience. My partner and I went to see Coldplay here in Las Vegas, where I live. It was a stadium show with over 60,000 people in attendance. What amazed me was how the band could take such a large crowd and make each person feel like an individual, while creating a sense of unity among us all.

One of the standout features of Coldplay's shows is the LED bracelets they give out as you enter the arena (okay, I know other performers probably do this, too, and that is not the point). These light-up bracelets flashed in sync during various moments of the concert, enhancing the magical experience of the performance.

But beyond the songs and the enjoyment of the concert, what truly struck me was the value they bring as a band. Just before the show started, a video played on the screen, showcasing how Coldplay gives back. It explained that a portion of every ticket sold is donated to various charities, including ocean cleanup efforts, support for endangered species, and assistance for impoverished children in developing countries. As a concert-goer, I realized that I was part of something bigger.

Coldplay's commitment to sustainability was also remarkable. They had bikes set up on the ground floor that concert-goers could ride to generate energy for the show. Additionally, there were trampolines that, when jumped on, also produced energy. I wasn't sure how the mechanics worked, but it was inspiring to see so many people contributing to this effort. While I'm sure other bands may do similar things, this was my experience with Coldplay, which made me feel valued while allowing me to contribute to something significant.

Another thing that amazed me and added to the value I felt at the concert was the connection with the audience. The way Chris Martin pulled everyone into the experience. There was a moment when the lights were turned on, and he took time to read people's signs, out loud. He recognized the various flags being waved from all over the world, flags even from opposing countries, and flags representing Pride. He said that everyone is welcome, adding value in its truest sense and, more importantly, making sure everyone felt valued. Yes, in a stadium of 60,000 plus, I walked away feeling *valued.*

Everything I share relates to adding value; in our discussions about personal branding or having heart, it's all about creating experiences.

As you read this book, you're having your own experience, and I encourage you to reflect on what you'll do with it. It's easy to do nothing, but from this experience, you might discover the value you can offer to others and the impact it could have on your personal brand.

Every experience you have shapes who you are and how you show up in everyday life. Each moment contributes to your belief system.

Ultimately, life is a series of experiences that create and shape the value you bring to others.

HOOKER HOMEWORK

What is the value you bring to others? Make a list of all the ways you can offer and share your value. We all have something of value to offer others. Sometimes, the best value you can bring is just being there for someone who needs you.

The value I offer is:

____

____

____

____

Everyone has their own set of values. Writing this book is a way for me to offer value to you, the reader. In the end, you'll believe what you choose to believe. You will do the exercises you choose to do. I truly believe there is great value in the many exercises and stories, and I hope they contribute to the value you offer others.

When you offer value to others, you're also presenting new behaviors, owning your brand, and showing up with heart. You get the idea (I hope).

As we continue through the book, you'll learn more about how to show up in a way that is more authentic to you. It's essential to consider what you gain from this and how sharing this information can elevate the value you offer to others, ultimately taking it to a higher level.

FIVE

KEEP IT ENGAGING

The "K" in HOOKER stands for "Keep it engaging." However, before we move on, I would like to clarify the distinction between "keeping it engaging" and "engaging authentically."

"Keeping it engaging" is the wow factor, while "engaging authentically" is the real factor. Think of it like this: keeping it engaging is all about the energy you bring, the spark that makes people stop, look, and lean in. It's fun, it's lively, and it gets people excited to be around you.

But here's the thing: energy alone can only take you so far. To engage authentically is what makes that energy matter. It's showing up as yourself, letting people see the real you, and connecting on a level that lasts. When you combine the wow factor with the real factor, you don't just get attention, you create connection as a Passionate Hooker!

It's about how you engage in conversations, adapt to others, and bring your ideas to life in a way that truly excites and connects with people. People often describe real engagement by saying things like, "I love talking to him; he's so present," or, "She always makes me feel like I matter." This ability to draw people in is genuine engagement.

It's magnetic, but it's also a skill that reflects how you present yourself.

To achieve this, consider these questions: Are we speaking with energy? Are we asking questions? Are we paying attention to body language? Are we truly present, or are we distracted and thinking about something else? Are we actively listening, or are we merely waiting for our turn to speak? This is where the tools and techniques previously mentioned are crucial.

Using people's names, pausing before responding, maintaining eye contact, matching energy levels, and adopting a curious mindset rather than a judgmental one, all create an environment where people are more likely to engage in conversation. That is what keeping it engaging looks like.

But here's the catch: you can display all these skills and still feel unfulfilled. You can charm a room and not truly connect with anyone. Why? Because your behavior may not be rooted in authenticity. People instinctively recognize when something feels off, and you can feel it, too.

The best form of engagement doesn't come from a script; it comes from your soul. I often say that while I may teach the same material in workshops multiple times, I have never taught the same class twice. I approach each session with the intention of engaging and meeting the specific needs of that group. Trust me, we have all experienced workshops or meetings where the leader just goes through the motions, which can be incredibly boring. People begin to nod off.

People often ask me how I keep my presentations engaging, focusing on my delivery techniques and my presence. However, I usually find myself discussing something deeper than just the mechanics; it's about the feeling.

One of my favorite films, which is also a Broadway musical, is *Billy Elliot*. For those who might not be familiar with the film, it's about a working-class boy from a tough British town who challenges the expectations of those around him by taking ballet lessons. In a pivotal scene near the end of the film, he attends an audition for the Royal Ballet School, which carries significant stakes for him.

Despite giving his all, he stumbles under pressure and, feeling defeated, begins to walk off stage. Then, one of the auditioners asks him a simple yet profound question: "Billy, what does it feel like when you're dancing?" Every time I tell this story, I get goosebumps because it resonates with me deeply.

Billy pauses in the dark theater, and he starts to put words to the indescribable force inside him. The song's lyrics reflect his feelings as he shares, "I can't really explain it. I suppose it's like forgetting, losing who you are for a moment, and sort of disappearing. Like you're part of something."

When he dances, he feels electricity. That moment moves me every time because it mirrors my experience when I start a workshop or stand in front of an audience. It's not merely a performance; it's something that resonates with my soul.

That electricity can't be faked. It doesn't stem from slides or gestures; it comes from the heart. This underscores how everything in *Passionate Hooker* is genuinely connected. We're revisiting the theme of having heart, which is truly about your authenticity.

There's a significant difference between merely engaging people and engaging with them authentically. When you focus on keeping things engaging, you consider your delivery, storytelling, audience involvement, and using your voice to maintain their attention. While that is important, authentic engagement goes beyond that. It's about sharing that electricity, your "why" and essence.

You're not performing; you're fully present. It's that true spark behind your eyes when you believe in what you're saying. It's the thrill you feel when you see someone nod in understanding because they finally feel seen. It's the current that runs through you and your audience when something real is happening. That's the current I strive for; that's the electricity I live for, and you can, too.

Imagine if we all shared that electrical charge; we'd be incredibly powerful. If you've ever wondered how I do what I do, the answer is simple: you have to feel something and then let your audience feel it, too.

HOOKER HOMEWORK

Here's a quick exercise to discover what drives your electricity. Think back to a moment when you were completely in the zone, fully immersed in something you love doing. Perhaps it was telling a story that made people laugh, giving a heartfelt toast at a wedding that brought people to tears, leading an inspiring team discussion, or dancing, singing, building, or writing something that made everyone feel alive.

The first step to pinpointing those moments of engagement is to revisit them. Once you identify a moment, write it down.

____

____

____

____

Now write down the words that express how you were feeling. Don't overthink it; just go with your instincts. You might write things like, *"I felt free," "I felt powerful," "I felt energized," "I felt connected,"* or even, *"In that moment, I felt like I was flying. Time seemed to disappear; it felt like it didn't exist."*

Describe that feeling and then identify the common thread.

____

____

____

____

What about that moment brought you to life? Was it the connection with others, the purpose behind your message, or the chance to be playful and expressive? The last step is to link this feeling to engagement.

This is where we bridge the gap between passion and engagement. Ask yourself, *How can I bring more of that feeling into my everyday interactions? What would it look like if I approached my next meeting or presentation from a different mindset, rather than following a script?* These kinds of exercises can be incredibly helpful.

When I feel _________, I am at my most engaging.

____

____

____

____

Now, why does this matter for maintaining engagement? Many people think that engagement is solely about what you say and how you say it. However, it's really about how you show up all the time.

In today's world, we are hyperconnected yet often profoundly disconnected. Engagement has become a form of currency. The people who know how to generate energy, interest, and presence are the ones we follow, trust, and remember.

Long before we held virtual calls, created strategy decks, or participated in employee resource groups, people gathered in tribes around fires, sharing meals, telling stories, and protecting one another. Love and belonging are essential for survival. If you didn't have love or belonging, you were vulnerable and alone.

Have you ever heard of Maslow's hierarchy of needs? I promise not to get overly research-focused, but this is important. Maslow's research on human motivation identified different levels of needs.

MASLOW'S HIERARCHY OF NEEDS

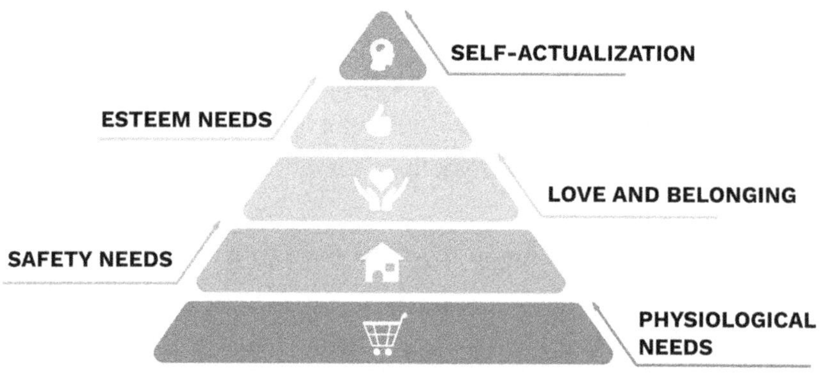

First, we have basic (physiological) needs like food, water, and shelter. Next, we need to feel safe. Above that, we have the need for love and belonging, which sits at the center of Maslow's model. He placed it there for a reason: before we can self-actualize and tap into our full potential, we must know that we are safe, loved, and a part of something bigger than ourselves.

In a tribe, love and belonging meant not just showing up; it involved participating, gathering wood, offering wisdom, singing songs, helping heal wounds, and engaging with the group. In the modern world, we need that same sense of belonging.

Whether we're leading a team, sitting in a café, or attending a family gathering, we all want to belong. Yet, we often forget something crucial: we cannot belong by remaining invisible. This ties back to owning a personal brand; visibility is a crucial part of that brand.

We build belonging by being engaging, which is why engagement truly matters. If someone feels like they don't belong or that they're not safe or accepted, they disengage. This isn't just about attention spans; it's about emotional safety.

Maintaining engagement is critical. Engaging others isn't just about being interesting; it's about inviting them in.

When people feel like they belong, they listen more closely, contribute more freely, and take risks. They ask questions and open up. We create a sense of belonging by using inclusive language, words like "we," "together," and "you belong here."

We can foster this sense of belonging and engagement when we make space for others to be heard, show genuine curiosity about who they are and what they think, and validate their contributions, ideas, and stories.

I recently came across compelling research that reinforces these points (thanks, Google). When people feel like they belong at work, they are more productive, motivated, and engaged, thus making them 3.5 times more likely to contribute to their fullest potential.[1] Another study from Harvard Business Review in 2019 found that companies with high levels of inclusion and belonging experience 56 percent higher job performance, 50 percent lower turnover risk, and 75 percent fewer sick days.[2] Additionally, the MIT Sloan Management Review concluded that belonging is the strongest driver of engagement, even surpassing recognition and purpose.[3]

When someone feels valued and part of something greater, you've already captured their attention—and perhaps even their heart. As a leader, your presence acts as a thermostat; you set the tone for the environment.

If you show up feeling distracted, guarded, or uninterested, don't be surprised if your team reflects those moods. However, if you arrive with curiosity and a willingness to connect, you'll see a positive change. Here's what engaging leaders do.

Before attempting to impress your team with strategies, impress them with your humanity. Learn their names. It's surprising how many leaders I encounter who, when asked about their team members' families, can't even provide basic information, sometimes not even their last names. This lack of connection undermines their leadership.

To be a genuine leader, offer authentic praise to your team. When people feel emotionally safe, they engage; when they feel ignored or judged, they withdraw. Our responsibility is to maximize the potential in every individual.

Engaging leaders avoid the burdensome checklists that often stifle productivity; instead, they inject energy into interactions. They start conversations with stories or questions like, "What made you laugh this week?" or "What surprising lesson did you learn recently?" These are not distractions; they're meaningful ways to connect that build trust and foster engagement.

Many leaders talk about their weekly team meetings, with agendas focused purely on processes, data, and deliverables. We need to rethink how we engage people during meetings and prioritize genuine connections. It's simple: genuinely connect with your people first before you dive into the process.

Furthermore, engaging leaders celebrate the contributions of their team members, not just the results. While numbers are essential, it's vital to recognize who stepped up when nobody was watching, who encouraged others, and who maintained a positive attitude. Acknowledging these strengths and efforts is just as important as recognizing outcomes.

It's crucial to help people feel they belong. Engagement isn't confined to a meeting or a team-building session. It's reflected in messages of appreciation, such as, "You did an amazing job on that presentation," or "I've noticed how much you've grown." Consistent, positive dialogue with team members is essential.

Remember, this is not just about leaders with formal titles; it's about everyone improving how they show up. We've all seen conversations where someone lights up the room, not by being the loudest but by being the most present. You don't need a promotion to be engaging; you simply need to genuinely care about people.

Every engaging person also asks meaningful questions. Instead of the typical, superficial "How are you?" ask something like, "What's been the best part of your day so far?"

Observe how people open up when you simply change the question you ask. I used to work in the food service industry, and I would often approach the tables I was waiting on and say, "How are you all doing today? It's great to have you here." Nine times out of ten, customers would reply, "I'll have an iced tea," instead of engaging in a genuine exchange or saying thank you. It was disheartening to see how disconnected people had become.

This experience highlighted for me how we often fail to connect with each other. Engaging people not only ask meaningful questions but also listen with their entire being, showing attentiveness through their body language, tone of voice, and choice of words. They know how to make others feel seen, often through something as simple as a smile. This is truly the magic they possess.

Engaging people also share their energy with others. They don't hold back their laughter or compliments; they generously share their joy, which is magnetic. They also express their truths; if they're struggling, they share that. If they're inspired, they communicate that, too. They seek connection and wish to be seen beyond just the polished images we often present.

I believe we all crave a sense of belonging, yet it's challenging in today's world, which is filled with constant distractions. We often ask ourselves who we want to connect with, rather than simply forging those connections. The most engaging people don't wait to be welcomed; they take the initiative to belong by engaging with others first.

That's the secret: if you want to feel like you belong, you need to show up as if you do belong. This isn't about faking it; it's about genuinely bringing your value, presence, and energy to the people around you. Imagine being part of a team where everyone feels important and valued, where people ask thoughtful questions instead of superficial ones, and where everyone is truly present, making others feel safe.

This isn't just idealism; it's about engaging in action. Whether you're leading a company, attending a dinner party, or spending time with friends, remember that your energy speaks before you do. That's a part of your brand. Your curiosity makes others feel valued, and your presence fosters a sense of belonging. Keeping it engaging is vital, not just because it's nice, but because it's necessary.

Think of engagement as using flint to light a fire (I learned that from the TV show *Survivor*). Your role is to ignite the fire, and your tribe is waiting for you.

We need to strive to engage more deeply with others, beginning with allowing ourselves to be engaging.

When I stand up to present, I truly feel that spark of electricity during my workshops. This energy allows me to confidently say that I've never taught the same workshop twice. I connect with the crowd and tailor my content to their needs.

While I know my material thoroughly, it's essential to engage my audience in ways that make the experience memorable. This concept, often referred to as experiential learning, has been around for a long time. Although it may not seem trendy or novel, many of us overlook its significance.

There's a big difference between simply showing up and going through the motions, like reading slides, and creating an interactive experience where participants actively engage in both teaching and learning, often without even realizing it. Being an engaging person is key, but it's also about applying that engagement to every aspect of your life.

We've discussed how engaged people show up. Now I encourage you to reflect on this: how can you be more engaging?

I want to share one more thing, as it's one of my pet peeves. Ever since the pandemic pushed us into virtual spaces, many businesses have started using platforms like Zoom and Webex. In every session, I always turn my camera on. I mentioned this earlier because it's crucial: you can't engage if you aren't seen. This is not a slam on any of the platforms; they are game changers and have created a unique way for us to engage. We just have to do better with the tools.

Remember, this simple action (being seen) is one of the easiest ways to foster engagement. Consider the moments in your life where you can show up differently, be more engaging, and become that spark that changes how others view their experiences.

As we move on to the next chapter, we'll dive deeper into understanding what authenticity means in the context of showing up and being engaging.

HOOKER HOMEWORK

List all the ways you can be more engaging. What are the engaging things you see in other people that you want to do?

____

____

____

____

Now that you have listed ways you can be more engaging. Write a list of what's holding you back, and why. It is important to recognize that those things that hold us back are typically in our control, and if it is in your control, then you can change them. So we can figure out how to:

____

____

____

____

Now, go out and do them!

SIX
ENGAGING AUTHENTICALLY

When I think about authentic engagement, I'm often reminded of that Dr. Seuss quote: *"Today you are you, that's truer than true; there is no one alive who is 'youer' than you."* This perfectly encapsulates the idea that there is no one else quite like you.

When you engage authentically, you're not merely performing; you're aligning with who you are. You speak from your truth, even if it's not perfect. None of us is perfect. You lead from your values, those driving principles that guide you, even when it feels uncomfortable. You connect from your core, not from a manufactured version of yourself or who you think you're supposed to be.

Let me clarify. Authenticity doesn't mean oversharing or being brutally honest at all costs. It means being anchored in your identity and allowing that truth to shine through when you show up.

Engaging authentically means being true to yourself. When I started my consulting business, ConleyGlobal, I was fortunate to have many organizations that needed me to work with their leaders and teams.

At one point, I was approached by a fairly large organization to collaborate with some of their leaders. Before they agreed to work with me, I had an interesting conversation that I believe is worth sharing, as it highlights the importance of authenticity.

During the call, the representatives made it clear that when I worked with their leaders, they needed to receive the level of learning they deserved. They expressed many sentiments, but there was one point they hesitated to articulate. I sensed something was off based on their tone and demeanor.

They hinted at their concerns, saying things like, "Sean, you have a great reputation, but, well, we're not sure you would be taken seriously. When you speak to our leaders, you can't be... umm... as... you know... animated." They continued to circle the subject, so I eventually stopped them and asked, "Is this because I'm gay?" You could literally hear a pin drop.

Immediately, they replied, "No, no, that's not it at all!" However, they acknowledged that the way I presented during classes, with my energy and passion, sometimes seemed a bit much for them.

What was really happening was that they were mistaking my passion, energy, and authenticity for something that didn't align with their brand image. I guided them through the conversation, stating, "What you're perceiving as 'too gay' is actually just my energy, enthusiasm, and passion." I emphasized that these qualities have nothing to do with anyone's sexual orientation.

It was crucial for me to call them out on this. The misunderstanding stemmed from their desire for me to conform to a mold rather than show up authentically as myself.

To be quite honest, that is not the kind of place I want to work, because I have passion and energy, and I bring that to everything I do.

This has nothing to do with sexual orientation; it's about how people can misinterpret my authentic self versus a canned persona. Everyone needs to understand that there is no one else like you.

People will often misinterpret you, your motives, and how you present yourself. We've talked about keeping it engaging. When you do, the effect is like an electrical current, the energy you bring, the presence you have, that spark that lights things up. It's about the need you have to help others feel they belong.

However, here comes the harder truth. If that energy and spark doesn't come from a genuine place, people will sense it. You can do all the right things: you can smile, make eye contact, and listen with intention, but you can still feel hollow or performative if you're not truly being your authentic self.

Reflecting on that situation, I realized that the misinterpretation was that my energy and passion were equated with something else. The truth is, this is my authentic self. I show up every day with that kind of energy.

To engage authentically means to be the same person in every room. It entails showing up with your quirks, doubts, and values, as well as using your voice. It involves refusing to mimic someone else's version of passion or engagement.

Authenticity is not about being perfect; it's about being real. It's about being you. Or, as Dr. Seuss said, it's about being "youer."

I hope that when I share this information, it conveys the right message, because there's confusion when people assume every gay person has an abundance of energy and that's how they show up. I have energy, and I show up this way because it's who I am; it's me being "newer" than you.

WHAT MASKS ARE YOU WEARING

Interestingly, anyone who knows me and has seen me on virtual calls will notice the wall of masks behind me. Nearly thirty years ago, I went on a trip to South Africa and was drawn to a ceremonial mask at an outdoor market. I saw it in the distance and navigated my way toward it.

An elderly man, weathered in face and hands, was there, and I told him how beautiful the mask was. He replied, "I saw you from far away; I noticed you looking at this mask. It is beautiful, isn't it?"

I agreed, finding the mask with its triangular face and large, closed eyes fascinating. The mouth appeared to both smile and warn at the same time. The mask had hair made of rope and hollow wooden beads, showcasing its beauty.

I didn't know why I needed to have it; I just felt I did. So, I bought it from the man, who told me, "It will always bring you luck." Now it hangs on my wall.

It all started with one mask back in South Africa. Today, I have dozens of masks lining the walls of my home and office. These masks come from all over the world: West Africa, China, Mexico, Korea, Central and Eastern Europe, Malaysia, Japan, Vietnam, the Philippines, and even one from a voodoo shop, purchased from a voodoo priestess in New Orleans. I could go on and on about my collection, but I think you get the idea.

Each of these masks holds a special significance for me. They represent places I've visited and symbolize my adventures and my life. Every mask is unique and comes with a rich story, shaped by different cultures and crafted for various ceremonies. Some masks were used in healing rituals, while others were worn during tribal dances to ward off evil spirits or channel ancestral wisdom. Some masks from the Venetian masquerade were designed to hide one's status or identity.

Years after acquiring that first mask, I finally understood what had drawn me to them. Masks across all cultures serve as tools of transformation, enabling the wearer to become something or someone else. They allow us to slip into different roles or identities. In many cultures, donning a mask is a sacred act, a means of connecting with a self beyond our everyday persona. However, in our modern world, we also wear masks. Not made of wood or paint, they are emotional, social, and psychological masks.

We might wear the mask of a confident person, even when we're unsure of ourselves. Sometimes, we adopt the persona of the agreeable team member out of fear of speaking up, or we wear a mask that says, "I'm fine," when we are not. Unlike the cultural masks on my wall, which were created with intention and reverence, the masks we don in daily life often emerge from fear: the fear of judgment, of not fitting in, or of not being enough or not truly being ourselves.

In the experience I just shared, people were fixated on the mask that represented what they considered my sexual orientation. When I showed them that I am a real person behind that mask, I was stepping into my authentic self.

This is why the term "authenticity" can feel radical to many people; it's challenging to grasp. To truly engage authentically, especially as a leader or in any relationship, we must take off those masks and say, "This is who I am. I'm not wearing a costume." This doesn't mean we have to overshare or delve deeply into our emotions all the time; rather, it means aligning our external selves with our internal truths and speaking from the heart.

I find it interesting how I keep making these connections back to the idea of having heart. Having heart also involves listening with genuine curiosity and owning our imperfections as much as we celebrate our strengths. The more I studied the ceremonial purposes of masks around the world, the more I realized that the bravest ceremonies in life are often those where we show up without a mask.

For many years, I felt inadequate because I didn't have a formal college degree. After high school, while most of my friends pursued higher education, I could only afford to attend a junior college. I worked two and even three jobs to make ends meet, having been on my own since I was sixteen. I didn't have the luxury of attending school full-time, but I did my best.

I know I'm not alone in this experience; many others are in similar situations. This is my story, my authenticity. Because I didn't have that diploma, I tried to work harder than everyone else. I aimed to outperform.

I tried to be more driven by how I felt. Throughout my decades-long career, I have pursued every certification I could find. At one point, I must have been certified in fifteen or twenty different behavioral assessments. I collected these certifications because they made me feel smart. I learned and taught several different coaching methodologies, believing that without a formal degree, I needed to gather these credentials to validate my expertise.

I read books and studied others, seeking knowledge for many years after high school, before finally earning a degree. I felt fortunate that I could apply many of my junior college credits and life experiences toward this goal, along with just a few courses to complete my degree. I thought that this achievement would eliminate my feelings of inadequacy and make me feel worthy, but guess what? It didn't.

Instead, my degree felt like a worthless piece of paper because I realized that my true education came from life itself. My most valuable lessons were learned through years of study, work, and gaining an understanding of people. That degree in life, my authentic experiences, is what truly defines who I am. It's not the degree itself that matters; it's your authentic life that shapes your identity.

Now, as I look at the masks displayed in my home, I don't see just artifacts; I see reminders. They remind me of the many roles I've played and the diverse roles we all engage in. These masks serve as an invitation for me to remember that they are on my wall for a reason. I am the person standing in front of the mask now, not hiding.

The most powerful connection we can offer others isn't a performance; it's our presence, our honesty, our heart, our brand, and how we engage with the world.

HOOKER HOMEWORK

My question to you is: What masks have you been wearing lately?

What would it look like if you took them off and showed up more authentically?

People are naturally drawn to those who present themselves without masks. Think back to when a speaker, leader, or friend moved you. Was it because they had perfect posture or the best slides? No, it was because they felt real, allowed you to see them as they are, and didn't pretend to have it all figured out.

Authenticity builds trust, and trust fosters connections. When you establish those connections, you can show up as the person others need. Whether you are leading a team or chatting with someone in line at the airport, being authentic gives others permission to be themselves. That's where real engagement lives: within truth, not performance.

However, being authentic can feel challenging for many of us because it often requires vulnerability. We are often taught to curate a polished image and emulate the people we admire. You might hide parts of yourself that feel overwhelming or inadequate, just like I have. Yet, those very parts make us compelling and unique.

Many people confuse being professional with being perfect, and a lot of leaders feel pressured to be polished, composed, and always in control. However, in reality, people do not strive for perfection. They follow honesty, courage, and humility—at least, that is what I would follow.

So, what does authenticity look like for a leader? It means showing up with clarity, heart, and humanity.

Authentic leaders speak from their values rather than from a script. They openly admit when they are wrong or uncertain about something.

These leaders lead with empathy instead of ego. I've encountered many people who equate empathy with weakness, but it is actually a great strength.

Authentic leaders create an environment where others feel safe speaking up and belonging. They treat everyone the same, whether they are speaking to the CEO, an intern, or someone working in the cafeteria.

People do not want a perfect leader; they want a real leader, someone who listens, shares, and acts with integrity.

When a leader is authentic, they give everyone else permission to be authentic as well. In general, authentic people may not always be the loudest or most polished, but they are magnetic because they are unapologetically themselves.

You know you're around an authentic person when they consistently show up the same way, regardless of the audience. Authentic people are honest but not cruel; they can deliver tough messages in a kind way. They demonstrate the balance between confidence and vulnerability. They talk with you, not at you, which is crucial.

Authentic people are comfortable with who they are, and they help others feel comfortable, too. Being authentic doesn't always mean feeling confident; it means showing up anyway and being grounded in your true self, even when it's challenging.

To help you become a more authentic version of yourself, here are some exercises that I have found useful over the years:

HOOKER HABIT

The Mirror Test: Before engaging with others, take a moment for self-reflection. Look in a mirror and ask yourself if you are bringing your true self into every conversation. Consider how you can connect genuinely without trying to impress others.

Get Rid of Your Mask: Choose one interaction each day where you consciously avoid performing or overthinking your words. Show up as your true self and notice how it feels and how people respond. This is particularly effective in the workplace.

Check in with Your Values: Write down your top three personal values.

____

____

____

____

Reflect on whether you acted in alignment with these values each day or if you compromised. Clarifying your values can significantly enhance your authenticity. You can also conduct this exercise with your teams. Various value card sets are available online that can help you identify your values.

Be Honest and Kind: When delivering difficult messages, be respectful and gentle. It's okay to disagree, but do so kindly. For example, you might say, "That made me feel uncomfortable," or, "I don't know the answer, but I'll find out." Being truthful, rather than simply agreeing to avoid conflict, is essential.

By incorporating these practices, you can embrace your authenticity and encourage others to do the same.

It's okay not to know everything. As I shared with you earlier, initially, I didn't know where the term "hookers" came from, so I found out.

One of my favorite activities is recording myself. Set up your camera and record yourself for one or two minutes, explaining something you care about without a script. Just talk from your heart. Afterward, play back what you recorded.

Ask yourself, *Does that sound like me, or am I trying to imitate someone else?* You want to be natural; you want to be true to yourself. Remember, the title of this book is *Passionate Hooker*, and you are the hook.

Don't waste time being a copy of someone else. Show up with all your flaws, your edges, your awkwardness, your unique laugh, your real opinions, and your full heart. That type of authentic engagement is unforgettable. We've all fallen into the trap of believing we need to be or act like someone else to succeed.

I shared a story earlier about how I was pressured to act like someone else (remember the "super-gay" story). I knew my brand and authenticity might not align with the image they were looking for, but I had to help them see things from a different perspective. Otherwise, I wouldn't have been true to myself.

You've likely seen charismatic people who are merely seeking attention. They aren't truly authentic; they're just performing. You might also have encountered leaders who effortlessly articulate their ideas in every meeting, leading you to think, *If only I could be more like them.* The truth is, when you try to be someone else, especially in high-stakes moments, you disconnect from your core, your center, and people can feel it. Your words may be correct, but something will feel off. The energy won't be the same; it will seem like you're just going through the motions.

Authenticity means doing things in your unique way, not in the way others do them. I remember coaching a mid-level manager who dreaded having team meetings. They tried to emulate their mentor/coach, who was a very popular vice president of the company. They were punchy, funny, and seemingly perfect. Despite all of these efforts, their team still felt disengaged.

One day, they told me about a breakthrough. They actually went back to the team and said, "Listen, I'm tired and cranky. I've been working hard, and so have you. I can't be the cheerleader today, but I believe in you, and I'm proud of what you are doing."

When they shared this, the team went quiet; you could almost see their jaws drop. Then one person said, "Thank you. That's the most real we've ever seen you."

Think about that: a leader who had been trying to be someone else and dreaded team meetings found a different connection by simply letting their guard down and being human.

On that day, they truly learned the difference between trying to be inspiring and genuinely being an authentic human. I love hearing about those breakthrough moments. I've experienced many of them over the years, but none were solely due to my coaching.

They occurred when people, perhaps influenced a little by my coaching, decided it was time to show up authentically. Ultimately, breakthroughs occur when individuals choose to be genuine, and that is the goal here.

HOOKER HABITS

Here are a few things to consider: Always speak in your own voice rather than relying on a script. Avoid using buzzwords and jargon that don't reflect who you are; instead, allow people to hear the real you, flaws and all. I often remind people that I don't speak perfect English; I speak like myself, and that uniqueness is part of who I am. I don't want anyone to imitate me, just as I don't want to mimic others.

When you present the real you, it becomes contagious. Your intention drives everything. Ask yourself, *Am I trying to impress or connect?*

Are you showing up to prove something, or are you simply being yourself? There's a significant difference between the two. Reflect on the "why" behind your engagement versus the "what." Understanding this distinction can make you much more engaging.

When I think about leadership, I visualize two types of leaders.

Leader A always has the right answer, never admits uncertainty, and maintains a professional distance. Their team follows instructions closely but rarely contributes ideas, making everyone feel like they're walking on eggshells.

In contrast, Leader B invites feedback when the team is stuck. They share stories and their failures, ask for help instead of pretending to be perfect, take risks, and create a safe environment.

These two types of leaders are everywhere. So, don't strive for perfection; strive to be yourself; that's the most important part.

When it comes to great human traits, I often think about the importance of pausing before speaking and being curious rather than overperforming. Embrace who you are, including your awkwardness and flaws; those elements make you unique. Authentic people can laugh at themselves; they possess humor and humility. They also maintain personal boundaries while seeking to understand others.

Here's a quick exercise: Write a paragraph about something you're passionate about. Read it out loud. Does it sound like you? Don't revise it; return to your authentic self and ensure you're consistently living your true passion.

One way to express authenticity is through creativity. Grab a piece of paper and draw something for fun, anything, without worrying about the outcome. You could draw a picture of your feelings, your team, or even the concept of authenticity itself. The goal is to unlock your creativity, as this allows you to be your true, free self. So, go out and buy a box of crayons.

Drawing pictures can teach you a lot. I have some great friends who are incredibly creative. Through their company, Another Limited Rebellion, they help unlock authentic leadership by encouraging people to be a bit more creative and imaginative.

Value kindness. A simple yet powerful way to express authenticity is to write a handwritten note. Yes, the old-school way!

Buy some notecards and write a handwritten thank-you note to someone. Be genuine about it. Those handwritten notes can really make a difference.

I've started collecting notecards from some of the countries I visit so that I have unique ones on hand. I also save every notecard I receive, as well as all the emails. I believe that going back to the basics and truly thanking people in writing shows them the authentic you and emphasizes the importance of being grateful. So, be more creative and kind to those around you.

Another important aspect I want to highlight is the value of courage. It takes courage to show up and speak up, even if you aren't sure of the answer or fear people might judge you for voicing your thoughts. Courage is essential.

Years ago, I had the privilege of seeing Anita Roddick speak. She was the visionary founder of The Body Shop, a popular cosmetics chain in the '80s and '90s. I attended her keynote presentation and stood in line for her autograph, geeking out with excitement. I had flown from Los Angeles to San Francisco just to hear her speak and get my book signed. When I finally reached her, she looked me in the eye and wrote something I've never forgotten.

In my book, she wrote, *"To Sean, be courageous; it's the only place left uncrowded."* At the time, I didn't fully understand that message, but I do now. I think about this whenever I recall moments where I've had to be courageous and risk my job because people misunderstand my passion and sexuality. Writing this book and sharing my words is a form of courage. I've learned that standing out isn't about being louder; it's about being braver. The braver you are, the more authentic you will be. I carry this message with me every day.

Strive to be courageous in everything you do, because that is where authenticity lies. Additionally, remember to show up with kindness and in a way that resonates with others so that they see the real you.

However, I must emphasize an important point: many people approach me and say things like, "That's just who I am," using it to justify poor behavior.

You don't get to hide behind that excuse. You cannot point fingers, slam your fist down on a desk, raise your voice in anger, or belittle others. Such behaviors reflect weakness, not strength.

Engaging authentically does not grant you a free pass to bulldoze over people or ignore the impact you have on others. It means showing up with honesty and heart, owning your energy and presence with intention, and leading with trust, kindness, and respect.

You cannot call yourself a passionate advocate simply because you are loud, bold, or blunt. A passionate leader demonstrates emotional maturity. They understand that being genuine and respectful are not mutually exclusive; they choose to show up with care, not just confidence.

So, if you're reading this and telling yourself that you're "just being you," you've missed the point. You must show up in a positive way at all times. That is what being a Passionate Hooker is all about.

SEVEN

THE THREE R'S

Think of the **Three R's—Relax, Reflect,** and **Reward**—as glue. They make everything in this book stick.

You've come a long way and learned a lot. We've discussed how to engage with intention, show up authentically, and lead with passion. However, becoming a truly Passionate Hooker isn't about working harder or constantly being "on." It's about finding your rhythm, breath, and humanity throughout this process.

This chapter focuses on slowing down and reminding you how to achieve sustainable growth. It doesn't come from increasing pressure; it comes from consistency, compassion, and celebration. This is where the three R's come into play.

The truth is, none of this will stick unless you're ready to change your behavior. In my opinion, real behavioral change doesn't happen just because you read a great book (like this one), attended an inspiring workshop (maybe one I facilitated), or felt motivated by a quote (like my "Seanisms" on LinkedIn). Yes, I've shared Hooker Homework and Habits in this book, but none of that will lead to change unless you're willing to take action. Change occurs through small, repeated, intentional actions—one step at a time.

Once you adopt this mindset, you'll set yourself apart from everyone else. Remember what I said before: the easiest thing you can do after attending a workshop or reading a fantastic book is nothing. Doing nothing requires zero effort.

I don't want you to be someone who does nothing, and I certainly don't want you to waste your time, so let's work on making the insights from *Passionate Hooker* stick. Again, the three R's are relax, reflect, and reward. These are not just a soft way to conclude this book; they are an operational framework for achieving real transformation.

Remember, behavior change is fundamentally emotional work. It doesn't start with willpower; it begins with willingness.

A few years ago, I went on a whirlwind trip around the world, visiting multiple cities and countries with back-to-back sessions and crossing many time zones. My schedule was packed with meetings and presentations.

I had promised myself that I would stick to my fitness routine because I was dedicated to being healthier and taking care of my mental and physical well-being. However, maintaining that routine while constantly traveling is challenging. Luckily, I have an excellent trainer, Derek (LifeUp Fitness), and I've been working with him for years. Following his advice and fueled by my determination, I packed protein bars, a jump rope, TRX, and resistance bands. It felt like I had more fitness equipment than clothes.

I often heard Derek's encouraging voice in my mind: "You can do this, but you have to be willing." With that determination, my willpower was strong at the beginning of the trip.

Then, on the third day, things changed. I was extremely jet-lagged and tired. Conducting workshops on little sleep is draining. One morning, I found myself at the breakfast buffet in a hotel in Rome around 5:45 AM, ready to head to the gym afterward, only to learn that it was undergoing renovation. Later, I discovered that "renovation" was simply code for "the gym never existed."

Nevertheless, I was still planning to work out. I had the right intention and was willing to do so. I was in line for breakfast when all of a sudden my phone buzzed with a workout reminder. At the same moment, I was holding a really juicy, gooey pastry, full of carbs, right? I looked at my phone and then at the pastry in my hand and thought, *I have to do something.*

When I talk about willingness, I'm not just referring to the idea of wanting to do something. You really have to be willing to make that change. Willpower is looking at that pastry and deciding whether to work out or eat it. But willingness is about getting real with myself and taking an honest step forward.

In that moment, I decided to stop aiming for perfection and instead aimed to be real. I put the pastry down, left the hotel restaurant, and walked out onto the balcony. From there, I could see parts of the city, and I made a promise to myself. I told myself that I was putting too much pressure on my shoulders. I had all my gear, but I also wanted to enjoy my food, so I decided to shift my mindset. Instead of going to the gym that day, I promised myself that I would walk more and drink water.

I felt so much pressure about hitting the gym that it had been making the experience not fun. I was torn between the desire for the pastry and the need to work out, feeling that the pastry would sabotage my workout. I realized that while my willpower was strong, it was willingness that I truly needed: the willingness to change and do things differently. When you think about it, willpower gets you to the airport, but willingness allows you to enjoy the journey, and maybe even earn an upgrade on your next flight.

Willpower and willingness are two different things. We need to cultivate the willingness to change and to want something different. To develop that willingness, you must let go of the protective patterns you've established. You need to embrace vulnerability, grant yourself grace, and try approaches that may not feel natural yet.

You might even need to be bad at something before you can improve. It's not just a brain thing; it's emotional, too. That's why relaxing, reflecting, and rewarding yourself throughout the journey are not optional, but necessary.

As we embark on this journey together, know that our habits won't stick unless we recognize that something has to change. We must make it essential for us to be there. If you expect perfection, burnout will follow. Expecting overnight results is unrealistic. But trust me, if you stick with what we've discussed and resist that urge for the pastry, you will show up better and adopt the healthier lifestyle you desire.

If you commit to the exercises we've addressed here, you will also start to show up as a person who is truly passionate about their goals. Don't beat yourself up over every misstep. Instead, try again, reframe your thinking, and look at situations differently. Build a new rhythm in your activities, ensuring that this rhythm is filled with self-compassion, small yet honest steps, and regular check-ins, and that it fosters sustainable new behaviors, not just fleeting changes.

RELAX

Relaxing is a remedy for our fast-paced, hustle-driven culture. It reminds me of a trip I took to India. I've been there many times for work, attending meetings and teaching classes.

On this particular trip, I wanted to stay connected with my clients on the other side of the world while also being productive. It was the usual whirlwind of "go, go, go". On the last day of my workshop, I had about sixteen hours before my flight. Typically, I would have filled that time with more work or tasks to complete. However, I decided to do something I rarely do: I chose to truly enjoy India.

I often tell people that while I've been to many places, I haven't really seen many things. Many people might relate; we're constantly on the road, and although my life may seem glamorous, I hadn't really experienced much. This time, I wanted to change that.

I went down to the hotel's front desk and hired a car and a driver. When the driver asked me where I wanted to go, I told him I didn't have a specific destination in mind. I didn't require an itinerary; I only had sixteen hours to explore.

As I got into the car, my driver was kind and quiet. While we drove through the bustling streets, he pointed out various things along the way and took me to see some beautiful temples. One striking aspect of India is the chaotic busyness of the streets. If you've driven there, you understand the haphazard driving, but somehow, it works well.

I was in awe of my driver, who navigated the chaotic streets with calmness and patience. We stopped at vendor stalls and explored different neighborhoods. Eventually, he asked if I was hungry, and I eagerly replied that it would be great to have lunch. He offered to take me to one of his favorite restaurants nearby.

When we arrived at the restaurant, he opened the door for me and said, "Enjoy your lunch." I then asked him if he could join me, but he politely replied, "Mr. Conley, it's okay. My job is to take care of you. I'll stay here in the car; I've packed my lunch."

I insisted again, saying that I would love for him to join me. After a moment of hesitation and checking his phone for some reason, he finally smiled, nodded, and accepted my invitation.

We entered the restaurant and sat down across from each other. What unfolded in that noisy eatery in the middle of India was one of the most memorable conversations I've ever had on a work trip. He told me about the dishes I was eating, how they were prepared, and which ones his mother used to make. He shared his favorites and what he cooked for his children. He also explained the regional spices and shared stories about his life.

He described his daily routine: working at the hotel for five, sometimes six or more days straight, and only going home on his days off to see his family. In sharing his life with me, we formed a genuine human connection.

I learned that beyond the culture, the people, and the heart of India, there's something truly magical about simply sitting down, relaxing, and connecting with others. Relaxing isn't just about checking in; it's about being present and engaged. It's about letting the moment unfold and surprise you.

For me, this approach is relaxing. You don't need to download a meditation app to find relaxation, although there are many great ones available. I personally enjoy using Headspace (shout out to Andy, who has the most calming voice).

What you need to do is permit yourself to just stop. Stop rushing, stop performing, and say to yourself, *Yes, I'll have lunch. Let's talk.* Or remind yourself that there's nothing more important than being present in the moment, right here and now.

When we stop trying to control every moment (by the way, you can't), we often end up where we are meant to be. This was especially true during my trip to India. Normally, I would plan everything meticulously, but when I decided to let go of the itinerary and just go with the flow, everything changed. Inviting my driver to share a meal with me was a pivotal moment.

So remember, if you cease the need to control, you'll learn that connecting with others often involves soaking in experiences meaningfully. Relaxation is not quitting or laziness; rather, it is a conscious release.

It's akin to exhaling after a long breath, allowing yourself to sigh and let everything out. That is the essence of relaxation. For passionate people, however, stopping can sometimes be the hardest thing to do.

By writing these down, you are reminding yourself of what you can do if or when you feel stuck, over-pressured, or just need to take a little break.

I often fall into that trap myself, constantly rewarding my stamina with a "go, go, go" mentality. However, I've realized that to be more present and sustain that passion, it's okay to stop. If we don't pause to relieve the tension that builds up, it will lead to burnout.

And let me tell you, a burned-out, passionate individual is not appealing. Instead, we want people who are vibrant and engaged. Changing behavior takes effort, but it shouldn't consume all of your energy.

In the corporate world, employees face immense pressure. It seems like everything tends to be labeled as "critical, transformation, change, priority, urgent, etc." Unfortunately, all of this often becomes just a corporate program or mandate that carries with it a lot of stress, leading people to compete against each other and feel the need to justify their roles. This is how teams fall apart and how silos build up.

In this environment, we lose the art of connection and the ability to truly relax and enjoy our work and our co-workers. I'm not saying companies do not need to change, transform, grow, etc. What I am saying is that it must be approached positively and with the well-being of the people in mind.

The real game changer occurs when people within the organization are included, allowing them to be part of the journey without feeling stressed. We must learn to take care of ourselves and those around us. During the pandemic, many companies prioritized employee well-being, but what happened afterward? Well-being was once again replaced with urgency.

In my view, companies that prioritize profit without considering their people will eventually see higher turnover rates.

If you want to transform while remaining a passionate individual, you must take ownership of your journey.

Beyond the corporate world, relaxing shifts you into a state where learning sticks and behavioral changes occur for the right reasons.

In this more relaxed state, you regulate your nervous system. This is basically how adrenaline works. I know it is more complex than this, but that isn't the point. Adrenaline allows you to stay engaged longer and perform better. Change and transformation are not emergencies; they are journeys.

As we reflect on these ideas, we recognize the importance of staying present and relaxed. We live in a world that is increasingly obsessed with speed. There's a quote I often hear: "Today is the slowest rate of change that you will ever face." This signifies that we'll continue to be busier, with more goals, meetings, and pressure to improve.

However, when it comes to building habits that stick, the best approach is to slow down. That's really what relaxation is all about.

Relaxation creates the space necessary for transformation and change to take root. When you're constantly in motion, you risk burning out. It's those quiet moments that truly matter: taking a walk, enjoying a cup of tea, or sharing lunch with someone special.

These deep connections calm your mind and pave the way for you to fit more into your life. I have practiced yoga over the years with my trainer and friend, Francisco. If I have learned nothing else, I have learned that relaxing doesn't mean giving up; instead, it's about nurturing everything you've learned so you can grow.

If you want to become a better communicator, start with your breathing. To engage more authentically, create space, and observe how you are performing. If you're looking to build new habits, take a moment to relax, so your brain can keep up.

You can't force passion or fake engagement, but you can certainly foster lasting change instead of sprinting through life. Throughout my corporate career, I realized that not taking a pause didn't mean I was failing; it meant I wasn't thinking clearly.

I've learned that slowing down and pushing pause isn't a failure; it allows me to grow, breathe, and show up better.

I encourage everyone to think of relaxation as charging your batteries, the batteries that power who you are and drive your behaviors. Consider exploring various relaxation techniques. There are countless breathing methods available online. One of my favorites is called box breathing, which follows a simple pattern: inhale for four counts, hold for four, exhale for four, and hold for four again. I use this technique frequently in tense moments.

Another practice I often engage in is taking thirty or sixty seconds out of my day to sit still. I once asked a friend who is a devoted meditator to teach me how to meditate, and they simply said, "Be quiet." That's the first step: just be quiet.

Try doing a body scan to identify areas where you hold tension and then stretch those muscles. If you find yourself sitting at a desk for long periods, consider standing up and moving around; it may feel counterintuitive, but it can help you relax.

HOOKER HOMEWORK

I suggest creating your own relaxation menu.

Ask yourself, *What are three things I can do in under five minutes to help me relax?*

____

____

____

____

What are three things that might take a bit longer?

____

____

____

____

And what's one substantial activity I could do monthly for a full recharge?

____

____

____

____

The essence of relaxation is taking the time to stop, slow down, and simply be. Have lunch with someone from a different culture, learn about their experiences, and enjoy the moment. Being relaxed enables you to show up as your best self, which is our true goal here.

REFLECT

Now let's talk about the second "R"—reflection. This brings to mind my time living in London. One day, I was asked to lead a workshop at a conference on short notice. I wasn't worried because I had a clear idea of what I wanted to discuss, and it felt manageable.

I was heading home when I ran into some friends, who invited me to join them at a local pub called Molly Moggs, located right in the heart of Soho. I'm not even sure if it's still there, but back then, at least, Molly Moggs was a drag bar.

After work, my friends and I decided to stop in for a bit. I had a presentation due the next day, but I thought it would be a fun break. If you've never been to a drag bar, I definitely recommend it. It's just a great time!

One particular queen that night had clearly lived a full life. Her face was a bit weathered, her wig was slightly tattered, and her outfit looked like it had come straight out of the seventies, held together with safety pins, hot glue, and desperation. Despite this, she was captivating. After one of her performances, she called out a man near the stage who looked visibly uncomfortable.

She said, "Honey, if you're pretending to be someone you're not, you're working too hard." The audience erupted in laughter, and so did I. That line really stuck with me.

The next morning, as I stood before a room full of executive leaders, I realized I had been over-polishing my presentation and sticking too closely to my routine. Although I wasn't worried about the presentation, having done similar ones many times, I noticed I was too focused on appearing perfect.

Inspired by the drag queen's words, I turned off the projector and put my slides away. Instead, I decided to just be myself. I shared the story from the night before, and the energy in the room shifted dramatically. People became more engaged and leaned in.

This made me question whether I was leading authentically or merely sticking to a façade, like the drag queen's outfit held together with safety pins. This reflection was a valuable lesson. When creating new habits, they don't always have to be dramatic. They simply need to be honest.

Whether you're standing on a stage in stiletto heels or wearing a corporate suit, who you are is far more important than what you do.

Relaxation gives us space, but reflection provides direction. Passionate individuals tend to go full throttle, but growth doesn't stem from constant action; it comes from understanding.

Reflection is where the real insights lie; it's where leaders gain wisdom. You start to recognize what's working and what isn't without trying to be someone else. Passion without reflection can burn out quickly. If you want to grow with purpose, you need to look back and ask yourself how you're doing. What's working? What needs adjusting? This self-examination is essential in my life even today.

While I've taught the same workshop multiple times, no two classes are the same because I'm always adjusting and considering what will work best for the audience. Often, we rush through things and skip this crucial reflection process.

I could easily have gone on autopilot during my presentation to those executives and stuck to my routine. However, by reflecting and discarding my usual script, I changed how I engaged with my audience, and that significantly altered their experience.

This process truly transformed my approach to teaching. Reflection isn't about overthinking or being overly critical; it's about pausing and examining what you've learned. So, what have you learned from reading *Passionate Hooker*? Ask yourself how you show up now and how you could show up differently next time. That is the essence of reflection: taking a moment to think deeply about your experiences.

Reflection is partly about how we accept and respond to feedback. There's an old saying: "Feedback is a gift." However, I believe that, in today's world, we are not particularly skilled at either giving or receiving feedback in the way it is intended.

This is an area where we can all improve. Feedback should be aimed at helping someone grow and develop, rather than serving as a form of criticism. Before I offer feedback, I always ask, "Would you like feedback on this?" I want to share my thoughts, but only if the person is open to it.

Building this habit can be beneficial, and we can even extend it to asking for feedback ourselves. This connects back to what we discussed earlier about personal branding, which relates to our reputation. The best way to understand your reputation is by seeking insights and feedback. After receiving feedback, it's important to reflect on what you've heard.

Take feedback in the spirit it's intended. Remember that people may not always know how to express their thoughts effectively, but there is usually a message underlying their words. For example, reflection might sound like, "After taking five minutes to think about that tough conversation, I realized I was more reactive than I needed to be." This kind of reflection has helped me become a better leader and improve my feedback skills.

Self-reflection is also valuable; it allows you to gain insights from others. However, keep in mind that if we don't act on our reflections or refine our understanding, we're likely to repeat the same behaviors. True reflection involves taking action. This is how amateurs become artists and good people evolve into great leaders: by constantly reflecting, refining, and considering how they can show up differently.

HOOKER HABIT

Here are some questions you can use to practice being more reflective:

- What's really working here?
- What felt awkward or off to me?
- Where did I act out of intention versus reaction?
- What can I try differently next time?

Just as I did after attending an event, you can ask yourself, *How can I do this differently? How can I show up more authentically instead of going through the motions?* Engaging in this kind of inquiry is crucial, whether it involves self-questioning or seeking feedback from others.

This kind of learning is not just theoretical; it helps you make more aligned choices in leadership and in your personal, professional, and spiritual life. By regularly asking yourself how you can change or improve on your journey, you can transform everything.

Consider creating a simple end-of-week reflection list with questions like:

- What energized me this week?
- Where did I disengage?
- Who could I use more support from?
- Who can I reach out to for help?

You can also invite your team to provide their reflections and answer the same questions for you. Additionally, consider asking your team, "What's one thing you learned from me this week?" Then reflect on their responses.

Make it a habit to regularly check in. I try to do something like this at the end of the week, but you could also do it daily or after each meeting. The key is to make it a routine.

For those who may not lead people directly, consider keeping a journal—perhaps call it a "Hooker Journal." At the end of each day, write down one moment when you felt engaged, one moment when you held back, one thing you'd like to do differently the next day, and one thing you've learned about yourself. Reflecting on these prompts will allow you to answer the questions meaningfully and genuinely.

If you don't enjoy writing or aren't into it, try one of the alternatives I suggested earlier, like recording yourself to see what you would do. Focus on those key moments: what you learned and what you want to do differently next time.

You could even create what I call a "Passion Tracker." This is a checklist where you note at the end of each day what you did, how engaged you felt, what you're working on, and what you learned about yourself.

Use the space below to get started:

____

____

____

____

There are countless ways to explore your passions. The questions you ask yourself can truly change everything. The idea is that when you relax and enjoy the moment and then reflect on your experience, you're on the right path to creating lasting habits that resonate with you.

REWARD

The last point is to reward yourself. Remember, you are worth it. It's essential to acknowledge your achievements, as many of us were raised to be humble and downplay our successes. We continuously move the goalposts, which keeps us striving, but passionate living is not just about striving; it's also about savoring those moments.

Let others and yourself know when you've done a good job. If we don't pause to enjoy our experiences, we miss out on the true essence of living passionately.

I love rewarding myself, and I used to do it by engaging in exciting activities, such as attending concerts, enjoying nice meals, or purchasing items online. I still partake in those things, but now, when I really want to reward myself, I simply take a moment to reflect on how hard I've worked to reach my current achievements. I appreciate my journey.

I still collect feedback: emails and notes from people who have shared their thoughts with me. Sometimes, to reward myself, I revisit these cards or emails because they remind me of the impact I've had on others. It feels rewarding to know that I've positively touched someone's life.

It's crucial to acknowledge our efforts; failing to do so can lead to burnout. Be gracious with yourself. If you are not, you may find yourself feeling resentful towards both yourself and others.

Often, we wait for significant milestones to celebrate, such as the completion of a project or a major transformation within a company. However, if you stop and reflect regularly and reward yourself for the small things, these moments really matter and deserve recognition just as much as the big ones. Don't forget that it's about celebrating the journey, not just the end goal.

A deeper truth in all of this is that, if you don't learn to give yourself grace and compassion, you won't be able to extend it to others. It is essential to take care of yourself and reward yourself in order to show up for other people effectively. When you lead or connect with friends and family, you will always connect better if you first nurture kindness towards yourself.

If we can't be kind to ourselves, there's little chance we can be authentically kind to others. I used to feel strange or guilty about rewarding myself, but embracing this practice has changed everything for me.

Now I treat myself with more compassion. At the end of the day, behavior change is unlikely to stick if we feel too much pressure. We are wired for those dopamine rushes.

You know that feeling you get every time you hear a ping on your phone or receive an email? There's science behind this; it's a true dopamine rush. We are programmed to see these notifications as rewards, but they aren't.

The real reward is how you treat yourself. It's not the email or the tweet; it's about taking a moment to acknowledge and reward your efforts, not just the results.

Consider how this might apply at work. If you attended a tough meeting that you didn't want to attend, reward yourself for showing up; you could have chosen not to go. If you found yourself in a heated conversation but managed to pause instead of reacting, give yourself credit for that; it counts.

Reward yourself for thinking differently. If you tried something new and felt awkward about it, take a moment to celebrate that accomplishment. I believe that doing something out of your comfort zone should count as a double reward!

This isn't about indulgence; it's about meaningful reinforcement. When we reward ourselves, even with small acknowledgments, we create momentum and teach our bodies and minds about the kind of person we aspire to be.

This is what a passionate individual embodies. Perhaps most importantly, when you treat yourself with kindness, you set an example for others to follow. Think about that: the way you treat yourself shows others how they should treat themselves, too. That is a profound gift and a significant reward.

Here are a few things to consider, whether you're a leader or simply anyone looking to make a difference:

If you're a team leader, consider starting your one-on-ones by highlighting something that person has done really well, no caveats, just clear recognition. Often, our team meetings focus on processes and projects, but a great reward is to genuinely acknowledge each team member. This recognition is beneficial for both you and your team, as it helps you see them in a new light.

When team members reach a milestone on a project, take the time to celebrate it. Bring in treats or organize a happy hour, whatever feels right to you. Show gratitude by writing heartfelt notes to your team members, thanking them for their hard work.

Instead of leading your meetings with project updates, start by discussing wins. Ask each team member to share something they are proud of. This shift can dramatically change team dynamics.

This approach is about making recognition deliberate in your team interactions. Many of us tend to focus on what went wrong rather than what went right, so it's important to shift that perspective.

At the end of the week, take a moment to write down what you're proud of. Where did you put in significant effort? Even if the outcome wasn't what you hoped, recognize your hard work. You might even want to create a personal reward menu, which can include anything from a nice meal or a cup of coffee to (if you're like me) a new hat, because I love getting a new hat!

Create your own rewards that encompass not only tangible treats but also emotional rewards. Additionally, strive to be kinder to the people you care about the most.

In my opinion, we often treat those people in the worst ways, taking them for granted. Simple gestures, such as telling your loved one they look nice or acknowledging their efforts, can make a significant difference. Instead of just talking about your day, ask them about theirs. Consider taking a walk with someone or even alone to enjoy the scenery and appreciate things like the sunset.

These are great ways to reward yourself. Another enjoyable exercise, which I refer to as "building a Win Bank," involves keeping a notebook to track your weekly achievements. From time to time, read these wins aloud to remind yourself of your accomplishments, much like I use my note cards. It's essential to celebrate your successes.

HOOKER HOMEWORK

How will you reward yourself?

____

____

____

____

You've likely encountered leaders who are kind and compassionate and who strive to say the right things. They want their team to feel valued, almost like family. While these leaders may be well-intentioned, they often struggle to achieve results or develop their teams effectively. They may avoid tough conversations or let toxic behavior slide, choosing instead to nod along in meetings without taking action. Although they mean well, they might not lead their teams where they need to go.

As the saying goes, "The road to hell is paved with good intentions." The truth is that intentions without actions are merely daydreams disguised as leadership.

To be effective, you must be intentional about relaxing, reflecting, and rewarding yourself. Otherwise, you risk becoming that superficial, overly nice person without any substance behind your actions. People remember what you do, not what you meant to do. So, cultivate intentions that lead to meaningful actions.

Understand that your actions matter more than your intentions. If you want to be a truly passionate hooder who engages authentically and leads with purpose, you need to ensure that your good intentions translate into courageous and clear actions, paired with a healthy dose of honesty.

To reach that place, it's essential to recognize that how you show up can change everything. Building certain behaviors, confronting those awkward moments, and having conversations you might be avoiding, will help you become a better version of yourself and a more effective leader.

Kindness is always important. Remember, you can be kind while also being direct. Your intentions must align with your actions. Be kind to yourself and to others. Our goal isn't to fix people; rather, we aim to be more authentic and true to ourselves.

There are many great resources on making positive changes, but I recommend keeping it simple. Take some notes to remind yourself of how you wish to be rewarded, how you have reflected on your experiences, and what you are truly trying to accomplish.

You have the power to change everything if you give yourself permission. This is what the three R's are about: creating meaningful change through relaxation, reflection, and rewarding ourselves.

EIGHT
FROM HOOKER TO HOOKERS

The first time I saw the video I call "The Crazy Dancing Man," I couldn't stop watching it. Maybe you've seen it, too—it's been around for years. It shows a man at a music festival, shirtless, dancing wildly on a hill all by himself. At first, he looks a little ridiculous, like that guy you avoid making eye contact with, but then something amazing happens.

One person joins him. Then another. And another. Within minutes, the hillside is filled with hundreds of people dancing together, celebrating like it's the best moment of their lives. Goosebumps every time I watch it.

The video is about creating a movement.

Passionate Hooker is my version of this video. It is about creating a movement of passionate people. It starts with one person willing to put themselves out there. One spark. One act of energy and freedom. But the real magic happens when the first follower shows up (that's you now... see what I did?) because that's when it begins to spread. Passion is powerful, but passion that spreads is transformational—it ignites a spark.

"S" IS FOR SPARK

Writing this book felt a little like that for me. The idea had been in my head for many years, but I didn't have the spark. When I finally found my spark, I sat down to share ideas that matter to me.

At first, it's just me on the page. But then one person picks it up (like you did). And another. And another. Each time, the spark grows. The ideas spread. The movement begins.

That's the "S," your "Spark." It's not just about one person. It's about the contagious energy that turns one Passionate Hooker into many Passionate Hookers.

FROM HOOKER TO HOOKERS

Up until now, this book has been about you. About how you show up. About how you Have heart, Own your brand, Offer value, Keep it engaging, and Engage authentically. It's been about how you Relax, Reflect, and Reward yourself so you can keep showing up with passion.

But here's the thing: passion that ends with you... ends, period. Full stop! Passion that spreads becomes movement. That's where spark comes in.

Spark is the bridge between a Passionate Hooker and Passionate Hookers. One passionate hooker is powerful. A whole group of Passionate Hookers? That's a force to be reckoned with.

Think about it: one spark is nice. But a spark shared lights up the night. When passion multiplies, when energy spreads, when more people step in with heart and authenticity—the culture shifts. Teams transform. Communities come alive.

WHAT COLLECTIVE SPARK LOOKS LIKE

- Energy That Multiplies. Your laughter makes others laugh. Your curiosity sparks their questions. Your courage inspires theirs.
- Confidence That Spreads. One person's authenticity gives permission to others to drop the mask.
- Shared Passion. When people connect around meaning, the work feels less like "obligation" and more like belonging.

I've seen this happen in my own workshops. Sometimes, it starts with one person who dares to open up, to be real about a challenge. You can feel the room shift. Others nod. Then they add their voices. Suddenly, the group isn't just passively sitting there—they're leaning in, building off each other, creating something alive. The energy isn't just mine anymore. It's ours.

Even in larger-scale experiences, this principle remains the same. Think about a Coldplay concert where the audience suddenly sings together, united by the music, lit wrist bands, and the energy. Or take Hands Across America back in the day (damn, I just dated myself with that one now, didn't I?), where millions of people held hands and joined in a collective movement. The magic is always the same: one spark, then followers, and then a movement that's bigger than anyone could have imagined.

That's a collective Spark!

HOOKER HOMEWORK

1. **Spot the Spark.** This week, take note of when someone else shows passion or energy. Name it. Celebrate it. Passion grows when it's recognized.

2. **Be a Sparkler.** Share something you're deeply passionate about with someone else—not to impress them, but to invite them in.

3. **Create Collective Spark.** In your next meeting, gathering, or even at dinner with friends, bring one element of surprise, humor, or energy that encourages everyone to join in.

HOOKER HABIT

Build the muscle of sparking, inspiring, and amplifying others. Make it part of your daily rhythm.

- End every meeting by recognizing someone else's contribution.
- Ask yourself at the end of each day, *Who did I spark today?*
- Keep a journal of "Spark Moments," and record when you see passion spreading. Revisit it when you need a reminder that collective energy is always more powerful than solo effort.

One person can be a spark, but sparks die out unless they catch on.

The "S" is the bridge from self to collective, from solo to tribe, from Passionate Hooker to Passionate Hookers.

I want you to imagine this: every person in your workplace, your family, your community, showing up with heart, authenticity, value, and engagement, and then sparking others to do the same. That's not just passion. That's transformation.

So, remember this: one Passionate Hooker makes a difference. A group of Passionate Hookers changes the world.

NINE
MY FAVORITE ANALOGY AND SETTING YOUR INTENTIONS

I would like to share something that has had a profound impact on my understanding of people and their behaviors. This foundational insight has made me more passionate, present, and connected, leading to many of the discussions in *Passionate Hooker*.

Imagine an iceberg. You know what it looks like: a small portion is above the waterline, while the majority is hidden below it. In fact, I use the iceberg analogy in almost every workshop I conduct. I often ask participants how much of an iceberg is above the waterline, and they respond with estimates like 10 percent, 15 percent, or 20 percent.

Typically, I respond by saying it's "a little bit," which gets a laugh. One time I was teaching a workshop on behavioral styles, someone raised their hand and said 12.5 percent of an iceberg is above the waterline. I thanked them (smiled to myself slightly at the very exact answer) and went back to teaching.

Well, the next day, that same person came back with a computer printout saying that between 10-15 percent of an iceberg is above the waterline. Therefore, making their answer correct and validating their answer. Well, I did say it was a behavior styles workshop, and I learned a lot about behavioral styles that day. I've been sharing that story for thirty years, but in my mind, it still remains "a little bit." Why do I mention this? I think it's amusing, but let's move on.

When we consider the iceberg again, the small part above the waterline (that 12.5 percent of who we are) represents our visible behaviors, our tone, body language, presence, and the words we choose. What people see is just the tip of the iceberg; it signifies how we present ourselves to others. It's related to our brand and what people feel when we speak from the heart.

The reality is that we are much more than our behaviors. If you've ever led others or simply lived your life as a person, you know this truth: what drives our behaviors lies beneath the waterline. Below the surface of every individual is what we call "life." This encompasses our stories, struggles, and roots—essentially, it's who we are.

At the deepest layer of the iceberg is what we term "experiences." These experiences include every triumph, wound, and moment that shapes our identity. They are powerful. My stories stem from those experiences, and they help define who we are. Every moment in life is an experience that contributes to our understanding of ourselves.

These experiences lead to the formation of the next layer, which is our beliefs. Our beliefs serve as our mental models, the frameworks through which we interpret the world. After having an experience, our minds ask, "What do I do with this based on what I know? What rules can I derive from this experience?"

Continuing up, just below the surface, lies our value system, or what I refer to as personal values. These values guide our actions and decisions in life.

These values shape who you are. They drive you and represent what you stand for. Although these layers are invisible to others, they are what influence your behaviors.

Think of the surface as the tip of who you are, the way you present yourself each day. Just as I've shared my stories, experiences, beliefs, and values, you also have your own experiences, beliefs, and values. These elements inform your behaviors and interactions with others.

At the surface, we are passionate about how we show up, yet it's important to understand that each passionate person brings their life experiences with them. We talk about becoming more passionate individuals, people who engage, connect, lead with heart, and fully present themselves.

This journey isn't just about saying the right things or improving your presentations; it's about understanding the entire person, the whole iceberg beneath the surface. If you wish to change what's above the surface, such as your behaviors, actions, words, or the impact you make, you must start by transforming your experiences and seeking new ones.

This entire book isn't a checklist; it's an opportunity for a fresh experience and a new perspective on the world. It encourages you to see yourself and others with greater depth.

As you read this, you may recognize some of this information from previous workshops or books. You might think, *I already know this.* If that's the case, I challenge you: what are you doing with that knowledge?

If you're reading this book, it suggests there's something more you could be doing, whether it's new to you or a familiar concept. Either way, I invite you to do more than just read. Take action. Implementing the various Hooker Habits and doing the Hooker Homework are choices you can make.

If you want to change your behaviors and show up as a passionate person, begin by altering your experiences. Initiate different conversations. Engage more sincerely. Practice being open and vulnerable. Share a story that moves you, adding depth to your personal "iceberg."

To create change, you need to have new experiences and then act on them. Remember, you are more than what others see above water. When you live and lead with intention, that visible part of you transforms, making you unforgettable.

Take a moment to breathe, as it's time for you to embrace your role as your own passionate individual. You've nearly finished this book, but more importantly, I hope you've reached the starting point for something significant: a shift in your way of living.

As I have said before, I thought I was writing a book on how to give better presentations, but as I delved deeper, the book revealed itself to me. It has evolved into something far beyond just presentation skills. This work is fundamentally about how we live, how we lead, and how we show up for ourselves and those around us. I've spent years pursuing this work across continents, cultures, teams, and various environments.

One thing I've learned is that how you show up truly matters. It matters more than your credentials or the degree you hold. It matters more than your presentation slides or your job title. How you show up affects how others feel around you, how much they trust you, and whether they feel safe enough to be themselves.

Here's what I know: most people hide behind a wall of masks, trying to disguise who they really are. I've done it myself. We wear these masks to fit in, seek acceptance, or portray ourselves in a certain way. We use them to hide our fears or insecurities, as well as parts of ourselves that we're still trying to understand.

The issue with these masks is that while they protect you, they also disconnect you from others. This book is about removing those masks, layer by layer. It's about being bold enough to reveal your true self and brave enough to stop performing. It's about living and leading with your whole self.

The term "Passionate Hooker" is not just a catchy phrase; it reflects my journey. After years of leading, learning, stumbling, and getting back up, I've discovered what it truly means to connect with others on a human level. I wrote this because I needed it for myself.

It gets me a little emotional to say that, but it's true. I've been the burned-out leader, the disconnected team player, and the person who showed up with a mask instead of being fully present. But I found my way back to passion, purpose, and a more authentic way of showing up that is both effective and humane.

The acronyms I created, HOOKER and HOOKER(S), were never meant to be clever titles; they're a behavior model: a blueprint for resetting how we engage with others and how we carry ourselves in this world.

So, why does all of this really matter? How you show up impacts the world around you. It shapes your relationships, influences how people trust and support you, and determines whether you inspire or deplete others, connect or disconnect, and grow or stagnate.

Passionate Hooker is an invitation for us all to step up in our lives, leadership, and relationships with more passion, clarity, and courage. You don't need a fancy title, a new company, a different job, or a new stage to start showing up differently. You just need the willingness to change your behavior, live more open-heartedly, and commit to being the kind of person who makes things a little better.

So, be your own Passionate Hooker. Don't imitate me; be yourself. The world doesn't need more perfection; it needs more people willing to show up with a little more spark.

Throughout my career, I have helped people communicate more effectively. However, the secret I uncovered along the way is that every presentation I give is a mirror to my soul; it reveals how I'm showing up and how I communicate. Holding that mirror up to yourself will help you show up differently.

This book started as a guide for being more engaging on stage, but it has evolved into a tool for shaping how I view things and how I want to share those insights with others. It truly is about changing behaviors, and that doesn't happen by accident. We don't just wake up more passionate—passion is a habit.

Authenticity is not something we simply become; it is a conscious choice we make. This book focuses on changing behavior. Its purpose is to inspire action.

Here's what I want to share with all of you:

1. Try something new. Speak up when you would usually stay quiet.
2. Ask someone how they're doing and truly listen for the real answer.
3. Offer your perspective, even if it feels risky. Too often, I hear people say after meetings, "I should have said this." You're right; you should have said it. After the meeting is too late.
4. Take a breath before you react. This is something I'm still working on, as I often feel the urge to respond quickly. Pausing can make a big difference.
5. Tell someone how much you appreciate them and be specific about what you appreciate and why.
6. Start your next meeting not by merely checking boxes but by connecting with people.

You need to try more, experience more, and practice more. You don't need to be perfect; you need to be powerful. You don't need to be fearless; you just need to be brave and courageous. Remember, you are enough as you are. You just need to show up.

I learned by observing others more closely, listening more deeply, and reading the room, not just for posture, pitch, and energy, but for presence. I discovered that what makes someone magnetic is not just their technique; it's their heart, humor, and the way they engage others. It's about telling a story and igniting a spark.

This realization led to the creation of this book. Being a Passionate Hooker means being a person who draws others in with passion, purpose, and authenticity. This is the kind of leadership and people our world needs more of. Whether you're leading a team, raising a family, running a company, or starting anew, you can engage people in something real, not with tricks or polish, but with genuine presence.

Throughout this book, we have broken down concepts like having heart, owning your brand, offering value, and keeping engagements authentic. This is your guide for passionate leadership, not a pursuit of perfection.

If nothing else, I hope this book reminds you that you matter. Your energy, presence, and leadership style have a ripple effect far beyond what you can see. Remember, you don't need a microphone to be heard, a stage to make an impact, or a title to lead. You simply need heart, awareness, and the courage to act differently tomorrow than you did today.

So, get out there and be a Passionate Hooker. Lead and live with a fire that sparks the flames in others. Trust your instincts. Approach others with kindness, be bold, be brave, and allow for a little unpredictability. Always remember that by being your authentic self, you give others permission to do the same.

I've shared a lot about my stories and how we've arrived at this moment, but these are just my experiences.

Now it's your turn. Do it differently.

You don't have to follow my path. Just share who you are. You have your own quirks.

You have your own challenges. You have your own lessons and your own leadership style.

You possess your own brilliance. So, be bold and magnetic, and it will transform everything you do.

Having built my career in the corporate world, I believe leadership needs more authenticity. We need leaders who can shift their behaviors and show up differently. For decades, we've seen leaders who give orders, talk more than they listen, and appear robotic in meetings, wondering why no one feels inspired.

Even with inspirational messages in our company values, no one cares because we don't embody those values. Leaders need to live by them.

People are truly starving for authenticity. They want leaders who care, who connect, who remember their names. They want leaders who ask meaningful questions and aren't afraid to laugh at themselves now and then. We often don armor and masks, trying to appear better than we are, when what we really need is to be ourselves.

Leadership isn't about a title. It's about energy. It's about how you present yourself when no one is watching.

That's the true test of everything we do. It's about how you make people feel when they're around you and how they feel after you leave the room.

If you take away anything, it should be that you don't need permission to act with passion. You simply need to choose to be more passionate and make that choice again and again.

I truly believe in the message we're discussing. Your passion is meant to be shared. It doesn't belong in a notebook, on a vision board, or locked in your mind.

As you ponder, *What if I did that?* remember that your passion belongs in the world. It belongs at the dinner table, on stage, in hallways, on virtual calls, and in text messages.

It belongs in coffee shops and during lunches. It belongs everywhere because how you show up permits others to do the same.

So go ahead, spark that fire, engage with people, and do it one step at a time. You will genuinely make a difference.

HOOKER HOMEWORK

If you've ever wanted to change your habits and embody passion, you need to modify your behaviors.

Whether you complete your homework all at once or revisit it over time, it's your chance to change your behaviors, grow, and express your passion. Here are a few questions to consider:

What does being a passionate leader/person mean to you? Take some time to write down your definition.

____

____

____

____

What is your mantra or rallying cry? (Think of this as your own Passionate Hooker motivators.)

____

____

____

____

What serves as your North Star? (Where do you want to go? Who do you want to be?)

____

____

____

____

Reflect on all the chapters of this book and ask yourself: which chapter or idea resonated with you the most, and why?

____

____

____

____

What surprised you?

____

____

____

____

What challenged you?

____

____

____

____

What felt like *truth*?

____

____

____

Next, evaluate where you are currently thriving in your life or as a leader. Be honest with yourself. This is an opportunity to recognize your strengths and discuss what you are doing well.

____

____

____

____

Think about where you want to show up more passionately and

authentically. This could pertain to your relationships, work, creativity, or connections, whatever applies to you.

Another question to consider is: which part of the HOOKER(S) acronym do you want to focus on?

- Have Heart
- Own Your Brand
- Offer Value
- Keep It Engaging
- Engage Authentically
- Relax, Reflect, and Reward
- Spark

Circle the one you choose to focus on and create a game plan around it. Why did you select that one?

For the elements you've circled, identify one small action you'll take in the next twenty-four hours to start building this habit. Remember, this is all about habit change. Think about how you can make it manageable.

———————————————————————————————

———————————————————————————————

———————————————————————————————

———————————————————————————————

Once you have a plan, take action. You might want a "Hooker Partner" to accompany you on this journey. Invite someone, a colleague, a friend, or even a new acquaintance, who can support you.

Consider another key question: What does success look like for you as a Passionate Hooker six months from now? Visualize it in your mind. How do you want to show up? How do you want to live and lead?

———————————————————————————————

———————————————————————————————

———————————————————————————————

———————————————————————————————

Finally, reflect on this thought: If you could leave just one lasting impact on the people you lead and love, what would it be?

____

____

____

____

Create a ten-day Passionate Hooker Challenge. Start small and commit to making a positive impact. Here are some ideas for each day:

Day One: Define what "Have Heart" means to you. Identify three values that matter most to you and keep them in mind.

Day Two: Check in on your brand. Ask someone what three words they would use to describe you, and compare these to your own description.

Day Three: Offer value without expectation. Do something nice for someone else without asking for anything in return.

Day Four: Find ways to be more engaging. This could be starting a new conversation or writing a unique email.

Day Five: Embrace authenticity. Share a true story with your team or loved ones.

Day Six: Relax. Set aside fifteen minutes to do absolutely nothing. Just breathe and enjoy the moment.

Day Seven: Reflect like a pro. Ask yourself what you accomplished this week and identify one thing you are proud of.

Day Eight: Take a moment to celebrate and reward yourself! Acknowledge a small win in your journey and reward yourself with kindness. It's important to recognize your progress, no matter how small.

Day Nine: Ignite the spark in someone else. Share what you have been learning and doing to become a Passionate Hooker. Share with them your journey and your passion. Be the spark they need to embark on their own journey.

Day Ten: Decide on your next step. What's one significant action or a small task that you will commit to in order to continue living as a Passionate Hooker?

FINAL THOUGHTS...

When I first sat down to write this book, I thought I was writing it for an audience: leaders, teams, and anyone who wanted to show up with more passion and connection in their work and in their lives. And yes, that's true. But as the pages piled up, a deeper truth kept tugging at me: I was writing this book for myself.

That realization was equal parts humbling and freeing. Humbling, because it reminded me that I don't have this all figured out. Freeing, because it meant I didn't have to. I could simply tell the truth about what I've learned, what I've practiced, what I've messed up, and what I'm still learning today.

This book, in the end, has been a love letter to myself (I am a romantic at heart). A reminder of the kind of leader, teacher, colleague, friend, partner, and human I want to keep being. But love letters are meant to be shared. And that's why I'm offering it to you —because if these reminders are powerful enough to shake me awake, then maybe they'll do the same for you.

DOING THE WORK MYSELF

One thing you should know: as I wrote each chapter, I did every single exercise. All of them. Not as an afterthought, but as a commitment. I wanted to make sure this wasn't just a list of clever ideas or nice-sounding phrases. I wanted to prove to myself (again) that this stuff works.

I remember sitting at my desk, drafting the "Have Heart" chapter, and thinking, *Well, Sean, if you're going to ask other people to do some homework and build new habits on their journey, you better do the same thing.* So I grabbed a pen and started jotting down my own answers, just as I asked you to. And sure enough, it wasn't just an exercise for me to build this book—it was a gut check. I found myself staring at the paper, reminded of what really matters to me, and realizing how easy it is to drift away from it in the noise of my daily life.

Later, with "Own Your Brand," I pushed myself through the reflection questions again. It felt almost silly at first—shouldn't I, of all people, know my own brand by now? But once I started writing, fresh insights bubbled up. Some were affirmations, some were surprises, and some were uncomfortable truths. That's when I knew these weren't one-and-done exercises. They were tools I could keep coming back to, and each time they would meet me where I was.

By the time I got to the sections in "Relax, Reflect, Reward," I'll be honest: I needed them. Writing a book is exhausting; it has truly been a decade in the making. But making the decision to work with a publishing company (shout out to the Game Changer Publishing team), this is when the work became real, and it was hard. I had to give myself permission to pause, look back, and celebrate my progress.

Doing the work alongside the writing was like having a mirror held up to me the entire time. It reminded me that these aren't just lessons I'm handing out, but they're practices I'm still living. Like everyone else, I have my good days and the days when I can't be bothered. Those are the days I know I most need to live the lessons in this book.

These are my lessons: Every idea in these chapters has roots. Some came from my own hard-won lessons. Others were gifted to me by mentors, colleagues, friends, or even a casual conversation that struck me in an unexpected way. And some I've researched, dug into, and wrestled with over the years.

But here's the key: I've done something with every single one of them. I didn't just hear them, nod politely, and move on. I tested them, stumbled over them, adjusted them, and kept putting them into practice until they stuck or until I learned something better. That's why I feel confident sharing them now, because they've been lived, not just written.

MY INVITATION TO THE HOOKER PARTY

If you've made it this far, then you and I are already connected. Maybe we've never met, but we are walking the same road (sometimes I can sound so profound), trying to live and lead with more heart, more passion, and more authenticity. That connection is why I believe this book matters.

I want you to know that I don't see this as a finish line. This isn't "mission accomplished." "Check the box." This is an invitation. An invitation to the Hooker Party, a party where you are the guest of honor, and you are invited to keep practicing, to keep experimenting, to keep laughing at yourself when you fall down, and to keep choosing passion, even when it feels easier to check out.

You don't have to get it perfect. I sure don't. But you do have to keep showing up.

STAND PROUDLY ON YOUR HOOKER CORNER

The HOOKER model isn't just a framework. It's a mirror. Every day I hold it up to myself, and some days I like what I see, and some days I know I have work to do. That's the whole point. Passion isn't a destination; it's a decision we make daily.

So here's my final reminder, to myself and to you: Don't try to be perfect (that's so boring), just be the best version of you that you can be, each day. Nothing more, nothing less. This book is my reminder to myself. And now, I offer it as a reminder to you.

And now... just for fun!

Wait! Stop everything. Just when you thought you were at the end, I have one more thing to share. Have you ever had one of those songs stuck in your head, and it is driving you crazy? Well, I got one to stick in your head now. I was listening to an '80s music station, and "Push It" by Salt-N-Pepa was playing, and I've had it stuck in my head ever since (thank you, ladies). So I thought, *Well, if I can't get it out of my head, I may as well stick it in your head.* But, with a few new lyrics (perhaps a collab in my future). And if you are too young and don't know what the heck I am talking about... look it up.

So I leave you with this...

The "Passionate Hooker Rap"

> *Ah, Hook It*
> *Ah, Hook It*
> *Hook it real good*
> *Everybody lean in, here we go now...*
> *The H is for Have Heart. Let it beat for everyone, let them*
> *   know you have a soul*
> *The O is Own Your Brand. Yeah, you know you're in*
> *   control*
> *Next, we Offer Value so connect and give back,*

Keep it super engaging, but keep yourself on track!
Engage it all Authentically. Don't be so damn fake
Now you know we got three R's. They're the closer, seal
*   the deal*
Relax, Reflect, Reward—that's how these Hookers play
Hook it
Hook it real good
Now you're a Passionate Hooker, proudly live it every day!
Hook it! Hook it real good!

WELCOME TO THE BROTHEL

And one final, final, final thing. I want to welcome you to the Passionate Hookers Brothel. Don't get nervous! We're not about to start singing show tunes or passing out corsets—unless you're really into that.

If you've read *Passionate Hookers* cover to cover, you now understand what it means to show up with heart, purpose, presence, and a whole lot of personality. You've joined a new kind of brothel, one filled with passion, courage, authenticity, and connection.

Thank you so much!

SOURCES

5. KEEP IT ENGAGING

1. TIG Advisors, "The Value of Belonging in the Workplace," *TIG Advisors*, 2021, https://tigadvisors.com/the-value-of-belonging-in-the-workplace/
2. Evan W. Carr, Andrew Reece, Gabriella Rosen Kellerman, and Alexi Robichaux, "The Value of Belonging at Work," *Harvard Business Review*, December 16, 2019, https://hbr.org/2019/12/the-value-of-belonging-at-work
3. Susie Lee, "Why Belonging Is Key to Building the New Workforce," *MIT Sloan Management Review*, June 13, 2022, https://sloanreview.mit.edu/article/why-belonging-is-key-to-building-the-new-workforce/

THANK YOU FOR READING MY BOOK!

Just to say thanks for buying and reading my book, I would like to give you a few free bonus gifts, no strings attached!

Scan the QR Code:

I appreciate your interest in my book and value your feedback, as it helps me improve future versions. I would appreciate it if you could leave your invaluable review on Amazon.com with your feedback. Thank you!